Captain Cook's
ENDEAVOUR

CAPTAIN COOK'S
ENDEAVOUR

CONWAY

KARL HEINZ MARQUARDT

© Karl Heinz Marquardt 1995
Revised edition © Karl Heinz Marquardt 2001

First published in Great Britain in 1995 by
Conway Maritime Press

This edition first published in Great Britain in 2001 by
Conway
an imprint of Anova Books Ltd
10 Southcombe Street
London W14 0RA
www.conwaypublishing.com

Reprinted 2003, 2006, 2010

ISBN 10: 0 85177 896 8
ISBN 13: 9780851778969

A CIP catalogue record for this book is available from the British Library.

Printed by Toppan Leefung, China

Previous pages
Left: HMS *Endeavour* at Botany Bay, 29 April 1770. Oil painting by Karl Heinz Marquardt, 1983 (now in possession of the Melbourne Maritime Museum, Melbourne, Victoria).
Right: '*Endeavour* at Sea' (British Library).

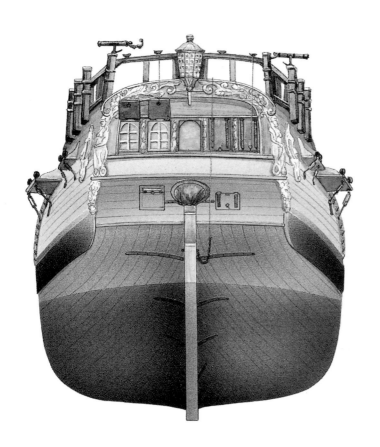

CONTENTS

Larboard bow of the Fremantle *Endeavour* replica at sea. Note the absence of the bumpkin and the fore course with the tack leading to the cat-head, which did not come into use before 1790. The reason for the built-in main tack fairlead block is obvious when looking at the main tack and chesstress. (*John Lancaster*)

INTRODUCTION

The age-old human urge to extend the boundaries of knowledge has always been a catalyst for voyages into the unknown. Thus it was in the 1760s when the Royal Society planned to send a party of astronomers to the South Pacific to observe the transition of the planet Venus between the Earth and the Sun on 3 June 1769, a rare astronomical event not to occur again for more than a century, accurate observation of which would add greatly to astronomy itself and consequently to the science of navigation. The expedition was supported both by Royalty, George III granting on 24 March 1768 the sum of £4,000 to defray expenses, and by the Royal Navy, which undertook to provide a ship. This was the Whitby collier *Earl of Pembroke*, purchased on 29 March 1768 and renamed His Majesty's Bark *Endeavour*. However, a decision still had to be made as to who was to command the ship and lead the expedition. The Royal Society's proposal of a civilian, the noted hydrographer and cartographer Alexander Dalrymple, was rejected by the Lords of the Admiralty as totally against all the rules of the Navy and a 'proper person' was selected instead.

This 'proper person' was James Cook, Master of HM Schooner *Grenville* and highly approved of by the Admiralty as a navigator, surveyor and cartographer. The choice of this 39 year-old warrant officer not only as the commander of the expedition vessel but also as one of the official observers has been proved to be the best choice Their Lordships could have made. Cook's three voyages of discovery in the Pacific put this part of the world firmly on the map and the name of his most famous ship, *Endeavour*, is, together with those of his later vessels *Resolution*, *Discovery* and *Adventure*, an outstanding memorial to an outstanding man.

Earlier narratives of the great voyages of exploration, concentrating more on the element of individual human achievement, neglected detailed and accurate descriptions of the ships involved, the means by which these great achievements were made. Demand for this sort of information developed only recently and much research still needs to be done, so detailed information on the ships of the great explorers is relatively rare. However, thanks to the British Admiralty's policy of meticulously recording the lines of all Royal Navy ships, either built, bought or captured, the *Endeavour* is an exception to this rule. Three sets of original draughts have survived, one depicting the vessel as purchased, the second as fitted at Deptford Yard for her historic voyage and the third after her return, when she was refitted for further service as a transport ship. The most important period of her service, her voyage round the world under Cook, is further documented in several journals, as well as in a few sketches by the expedition's botanical artist Sydney Parkinson.

Reconstruction of such a well-documented ship, one would assume, would not give rise to the flights of fancy that often occur with other well-known, but less well-documented, vessels. However, an exhaustive study of the original draughts, together with J C Beaglehole's *The Journals of Captain James Cook Vol. 1: The Voyage of the Endeavour 1768-1771* and other contemporary works of a more general nautical nature, has shown this not to be the case.

Few ships in history have fascinated model makers as much as the *Endeavour*, and countless models, as well as some full-size replicas, have been built by amateurs and professionals alike, many being accepted as permanent exhibits by highly reputable museums around the world, some of which are shown in the photographic section of this book. However, none of these sometimes superbly crafted miniature *Endeavour*s have done much to advance our still largely superficial knowledge beyond the point of the well-known model plans of many decades ago. The situation has improved recently with the launching of a full-size replica of *Endeavour* at Fremantle, Western Australia, which has the four stern windows and their dead-lights,[1] as well as certain items of deck furniture. However, as regards the fitting of bumpkins, the length of the mizzenmast and several other points, the designer has chosen to keep to the traditional image of the *Endeavour*. This view of *Endeavour* is based on the original draughts, but the rigging and furnishing details are drawn from contemporary nautical knowledge, the results of which are not in accordance with the information in the *Endeavour* journals and have created a distorted picture of the actual ship.

Thorough examination of these journals and the draughts reveals a mine of previously unused primary source information, upon which the following drawing work has been based. Therefore these drawings do not entirely comply with existing well-known models and reconstruction drawings. These previously overlooked details will be explained both in the drawings and the text, by reference to the contemporary sources, so that past misconceptions may be corrected. These misconceptions range

---

1. K H Marquardt, 'Do we really know the *Endeavour*?', *The Great Circle* Vol 8, No 1 1986; K H Marquardt, 'HM Bark *Endeavour* , what do we really know about the ship?' *Nautical Research Journal* Vol 35, No 1 (1990).

from the treatment of the hull below the waterline to the controversies surrounding the stern windows, a shorter than normal mizzen mast and the bumpkins. The evidence for the correction of these misconceptions will be presented in the following sections.

Ship's history

June 1764: Built by Thomas Fishburn at Whitby as the *Earl of Pembroke*. Employed in the coal trade.

1768

Mar: For sale on the River Thames, by her owner Thomas Milner.

21 Mar: Earmarked by the Navy Board. 'The Board suggests a cat-built vessel, which would be roomy enough for the purpose. One of about 350 tons can be purchased on the River Thames'.

23 Mar: Order to survey the *Valentine*, the *Earl of Pembroke* and the *Ann and Elizabeth*.

29 Mar: 'A Cat-built Bark in Burthen 368 Tons, 3 years 9 months old, has been purchased. In what name is she to be registered?' The price was £2,212 15s 6d for the hull and £94 10s 0d for masts and spars, which was later reduced to £56 17s 10d.

31 Mar: Master Attendant and pilot brought the *Earl of Pembroke* from Mr Birds' Ways to Deptford Dockyard to have her dismasted and docked.

2 Apr: Docked.

5 Apr: Registered on the Navy List as a Bark by the name of *Endeavour*.

25 Apr: The officers of HM Yard at Deptford said the Bark *Endeavour* would be ready to receive her crew next week.

Early May: Delay because of strike on the waterfront.

18 May: Released from the single dock and moved into the basin for finishing work.

25 May: A decision was reached to have the *Endeavour* manned by seventy men and that Mr James Cook be appointed to command her with the rank of First Lieutenant.

27 May: Lieutenant James Cook hoisted his pennant at 11am and took charge of the *Endeavour*.

31 May: Stepping of the lower masts.

18 June: Pilot took charge and HM Bark *Endeavour* set sail for Galleons Reach to receive her ordnance.

30 June: Weighed anchor and sailed to the Downs. Pilot dismissed on 7 August.

22 July: Cook was informed that besides Mr Charles Green and his servant, Joseph Banks Esq. and his suite of eight people will sail with him and will have to be accommodated.

3 Aug: A decision was made to increase the *Endeavour*'s complement to eighty-five men, including twelve marines.

8 Aug: Sailed for Plymouth.

14 Aug: Arrived at Plymouth in the evening to receive further supplies.

16 Aug: Additional crew came aboard.

17 Aug: Work commenced on the refitting of the gentlemen's cabins and the building of a platform over the tiller.

18 Aug: Another four guns and stores taken aboard.

20 Aug: Preparations for sea, delayed for several days by a storm.

26 Aug: Sailed with ninety-four men aboard.

30 Aug: Very hard gale. 'Washed over board a small boat . . . and drown'd between 3 and 4 dozen of our poultry'.

14 Sept: Anchoring at Plymouth in Funchal Road, Madeira, Master's mate Weir drowned. Impressed J Thurman from a New York sloop.

19 Sept: Departed Funchal Road. Two watch routine changed to three watches.

26 Oct: Crossed the Equator.

14 Nov: Arrived in Rio de Janeiro. Ship boot-topped and all necessary repairs carried out.

20 Nov: The longboat carrying four pipes of rum sank, but was recovered.

2 Dec: Intended date of departure from Rio. The seaman Peter Flower fell over board and drowned. Hired a Portuguese seaman as replacement.

7 Dec: The *Endeavour* finally left that inhospitable place. Pilot dismissed.

17 Dec: Watch condition changed back to watch and watch about.

22 Dec: A new suit of sails was bent and the top rigging set up.

25 Dec: 'Christmas Day; all good Christians that is to say all hands get abominably drunk so that at night there was scarce a sober man in the ship' (J Banks).

1769

6 Jan: Issue of warm clothes (a Fearnought jacket and a pair of trousers) to each man.

16 Jan: Anchored in the Bay of Success to take in wood and water. Mr Banks and several men went on land to gather plants etc. Unable to come back the same day and Thomas Richmond and George Dorlton, two negro servants, froze to death overnight.

18 Jan: Lowered the six main deck carriage guns into the hold in preparation for rounding Cape Horn.

20 Jan: Completed taking on water and wood. Lost a kedge anchor.

21 Jan: Departure.

25 Jan: Rounded Cape Horn in relatively good weather.

31 Jan/2 Feb: After first being used on the 23rd, studding sails were again set. The next day Joseph Banks was allowed to row his skiff around the ship to shoot birds.

16 Feb: A very heavy sea carried away the driver boom including the lee rails to which it was lashed.

12 Mar: Return to three watches. As a precaution for an expected meeting with islanders the six waist guns were remounted.

26 Mar: Marine William Greenslade was caught stealing and jumped or fell over board and drowned.

4 Apr: Land was first sighted (an island of the Tuamotus).

13 Apr: Arrival at Tahiti

17 Apr: Alexander Buchan, landscape artist in Banks' retinue, died of epilepsy.

18 Apr: Construction of Fort Venus.

29 Apr: Mounted two of the four extra 4-pounder guns on the quarter-deck and two at Fort Venus.

25 May: Longboat's bottom found to be completely worm-eaten and was repaired.

1 June: Lt Gore, Dr Monkhouse and Mr Spöring sent in the longboat to Moorea to observe the transit of Venus.

2 June: Lt Hicks, Mr Clerk, Mr Pickersgill and Mr Saunders sent to another spot to observe the transition.

3 June: Observation of Venus' transition across the sun.

7 - 9 June: Boot-topped both sides of the ship.

18 June: Observed a total eclipse of the moon.

Beginning of July: Preparations for departure from Tahiti.

9 July: Marines Clement Webb and Samuel Gibson deserted.

11 July: Deserters back on board. Punished with twenty lashes.

12 July: Anchor stocks were found to be worm-eaten and had to be replaced.

13 July: Departure from Tahiti with the Tahitian Chief Tupia and his servant aboard.

17 July: Discovery of the island of Huahine.

21 July: Landed on Ulietea and took possession in the name of His Majesty.

22 July: Surveyed the island and sounded the harbour. Investigated and surveyed the Society Islands.

9 Aug: Departure.

24 Aug: Bad weather: fresh provisions (hogs and fowl) died in the colder latitudes.

28 Aug: Boatswain's mate John Reading died from excessive drinking.

2 Sept: Tempestuous winds and increasing cold at latitude 40° forced the ship to turn back.

7 Oct: The North Island of New Zealand was sighted.

9 Oct: Landed at Poverty Bay and encountered hostile Maoris. Several Maoris were killed.

21/24 Oct: Took in fresh water and wood at Anaura Bay.

25 Oct: Repaired the tiller brace.

22 Nov: A native took the half-hour glass out of the binnacle and received a dozen lashes with the cat-o'-nine-tails.

6 Dec: A near-disaster when *Endeavour* unexpectedly struck a rock, but no damage caused.

9/31 Dec: Rounded the North Cape of New Zealand.

28 Dec: Struck by a hurricane and laid to under a balanced mizzen and mizzen staysail.

1770

15 Jan: After sailing down the west side of the North Island, entered Queen Charlotte Sound for repair of the tiller brace, boot-topping and for wood and water.

6 Feb: Sailed, nearly foundering on the rocks through tidal change.

11 Feb: Completed circumnavigation of North Island at Cape Turn-again and sailed southward.

25 Feb: Lost the main topgallant mast and a fore topmast studding sail boom in a four-day gale: a fore course and a main topsail were split apart.

March/Apr: Sails had become increasingly defective. The spritsail topsail condemned and used for repair material. Used tent canvas to repair jib.

27 Mar: Circumnavigated the South Island and headed again for Queen Charlotte's Sound. Anchored in Admiralty Bay to replenish water and supply of firewood.

31 Mar: Planning their return to England. Ship's condition too poor for the direct route via Cape Horn preferred by Cook or the direct route to Cape of Good Hope during the southern winter. Decided to return via the East Indies, sailing westward and then north along the east coast of New Holland.

19 Apr: Landfall on the south-eastern coastline of Australia. Named Point Hicks after Lt Hicks who sighted it first.

29 Apr: First landing at Botany Bay.

1 May: Able Seaman Forby Sutherland died of tuberculosis.

6 May: Left Botany Bay and sailed north.

22 May: Anchored in Bustard Bay. Captain's clerk Richard Orton was the victim of a prank. Somebody cut the clothes off his back and part of both ears while he was asleep. Midshipman Patrick Saunders, under suspicion, was demoted.

29 May: Anchored in an inlet to replenish water and have the ship's bottom cleaned. Not finding any fresh water they left and named the place Thirsty Sound.

11 June: Struck the Great Barrier Reef and made much water. To lighten the ship as fast as possible, the six waist guns were thrown over board, together with about 40 to 50 tons of other ballast etc.

12 June: After 24 hours of anguish, with everybody, including the Captain and gentlemen, manning the pumps vigorously, the ship was heaved off the reef. Lost the small bower anchor. Got up the fore topmast and the fore yard and moved towards land.

13 June: Fothered the leak, got up the main topmast and main yard and continued toward land.

14 June: Anchored 1 mile off shore from a possible harbour for repair.

17 June: After 2 days of strong wind moved into the river and ran on to a sandbank.

18 June: Warped the ship off the bank and moored her alongside a steep beach. Pitched two tents, landed all the sick and the stores.

22 June: Having landed all the stores and lightened the ship forward, the ship was moved up stream to a more suitable place to beach the fore ship.

27 June: After underwater repairs completed, tried without success to float the ship's bow with thirty-eight large empty casks.

4 July: Ship refloated and trimmed. Inspected next day to see if still making water.

20 July: Moved everything back on board. The ship now ready to sail at the first opportunity.

1 Aug: Pumps overhauled, as all in a state of decay, with one falling to pieces.

5 Aug: Departure from Endeavour River. With only 3 months' worth of provisions left and in danger of being locked in by reefs and shoals, it was resolved to make for the open sea through one of the channels discovered.

15 Aug: Steering west again for fear of missing the passage between Australia and New Guinea.

16 Aug: Land was sighted with breakers over a long reef and only a small channel visible. A sudden wind change pressed the ship 80 to 100 metres close to the reef. With longboat and yawl towing and the assistance of sweeps the bow was swung around and a slight wind change gave temporary relief. With tidal change and the help of their boats, the ship was safely navigated through this channel, which was only ¼ mile wide to an anchorage inside the reef. Being the narrowest escape from destruction so far, the place was named the Providential Channel.

19 Aug: Sailed again and 3 days later found a strait between New Holland and New Guinea.

22 Aug: Landed on an island and, in the name of His Majesty King George III, took possession of the whole east coast of New Holland by the name of New South Wales. The island was named Possession Island and the Strait is now known as Endeavour Straits.

24 Aug: Lost the large bower anchor, recovered it again 24 hours later, and had another narrow escape from shipwreck.

29 Aug: Reached the coast of New Guinea. Although the water was not deep enough for going close to shore, James Cook, Joseph Banks and Dr Solander agreed to set foot at least once in that country.

18 Sept: Anchored at Savu and bought nine buffaloes, a number of fowls and 'a large quantity of syrrup'.

21 Sept: Departed from Savu.

30 Sept: Arrived near Java Heads.

12 Oct: Anchored in Batavia Road. Up to then none of the ship's company was on the sick list.

18 Oct: Moved to Cooper's Island to unrig the ship.

23 Oct: Hauled alongside a wharf to clear the ship of all stores etc.

5 Nov: Transported the ship to Onrust for careening.

6 Nov: Yard officers took over the ship.

7 Nov: The ship's surgeon William Monkhouse died after a short illness. Several of the crew fell ill.

9 Nov: Ship careened. Her bottom in a worse condition than expected. False keel lost within 20ft of the sternpost, main keel on many places considerably damaged, much sheathing lost and several planks badly damaged. It was a wonder that the ship could have sailed such a long distance in that condition. Most of the ship's crew already sick and no more than twenty officers and men fit for duty.

14 Nov: Careening completed.

15 Nov to 7 Dec: Sailed to Coopers Island to take in all the stores, and to be rigged etc. Seldom more than fourteen hands able to work.

8 Dec: Departed for Batavia Road.

11 Dec to 24 Dec: Took on water and provisions and prepared the ship for sea.

25 Dec: Minor dispute with the Dutch authorities over a runaway Englishman, who took refuge aboard. Former midshipman Patrick Saunders deserted in a shore boat.

26 Dec: Departed Batavia with more than forty sick. Six people died during their stay. The surgeon W Monkhouse, Able Seamen P Rearden and J Woodworth, Charles Green's servant J Reynolds and the two Tahitians Tupia and his servant Tarheto. Nineteen new crew members were mustered.

1771

6 Jan: Anchored off Princes Island to replenish wood and water and to buy more fresh food.

15 Jan: Left the island and on their way to Cape of Good Hope. A journey of much illness and death, which Cook attributed to the water taken on at Princes Island. The list of the lives lost is long.

24 Jan: J Truslove, Marine corporal.

25 Jan: H D Spöring, Assistant naturalist.

27 Jan: S Parkinson, natural history artist, J Ravenhill, Sailmaker.

29 Jan: C Green, Astronomer.

30 Jan: S Moody, F Hate, two of the Carpenter's crew.

31 Jan: J Thompson, Ship's cook, B Jordan, Carpenter's mate, J Nicholson and A Wolfe, Seamen.

2 Feb: D Roberts, Gunner's servant.

3 Feb: J Thurman, Sailmaker's assistant.

4 Feb: J Bootie, Midshipman, J Gathrey, Boatswain.

6 Feb: J Monkhouse, Midshipman (brother of surgeon).

12 Feb: J Satterly, Carpenter.

14 Feb: A Lindsay, Seaman.

15 Feb: D Preston, Marine.

21 Feb: A Simpson, Seaman.

27 Feb: H Jeffs, E Pharah, P Morgan, Seamen.

1 Mar: The fore topsail sheet bits were worked loose by the bowsprit. Repaired as well as the situation permitted.

6 Mar: Land was sighted nearby at first light. Had to tack for several hours not to be driven on to the rugged coast of South Africa.

13 Mar: Passed the Cape of Good Hope.

14 Mar: Anchored off Cape Town.

15 Mar: Moved twenty-eight sick crew members ashore for recuperation. R Thomas, Seaman, died.

4 Apr: J Lorrain, Seaman, died.

7 Apr: J Dozey, Seaman, died.

13 Apr: Having completed all repairs, watering and provisioning, the sick returned and the ship was made ready for sea.

16 Apr: Weighed anchor and left Cape Town. The ship's master Robert Molyneux died.

29 Apr: Completed a circumnavigation of the globe by crossing the Greenwich Meridian.

1 May: Anchored in the Road before James Fort, St Helena.

5 May: Accompanied a returning fleet of Indiamen for three weeks.

24 May: Overtook the returning fleet.

26 May: *Endeavour*'s second ranking officer Lt Zachary Hicks died after a long illness

30 May: A new main topmast backstay had to be fitted.

22 June: Spotted the Indiamen fleet again.

23 June: Had both weather backstays broken and the main topmast sprung at the cap. The rigging was so bad that something gave way every day.

10 July: Lands End was sighted.

13 July: *Endeavour* anchored in the Downs. James Cook handed the ship over to J Hudson, the pilot and went to London.

16 July: Pilot brought the ship to Galleons Reach and left.

18 July: *Endeavour* to be paid off at Woolwich, but not dismantled more than absolutely necessary, as she would probably soon be needed as a store ship.

25 July: *Endeavour* to be docked at Woolwich, resheathed and fitted in all respects to carry a supply of provisions and stores to the Falkland Islands.

8 Aug: Lieutenant James Gordon to command the *Endeavour* at Woolwich.

16 Oct: Date on draught of the ship's conversion to store ship.

5 Dec: Sailed for the Falkland Islands.

1772

3 Aug: Arrived at Spithead from the Falkland Islands.

1774

16 Aug: Arrived at Portsmouth bringing home the Falkland Islands garrison and all the stores which could be loaded. She left the British flag flying. On her way home the ship's master Mr Allen and two men were washed overboard.

1775

17 Mar: Sold from the service.

1790

Sold at Dunkirk and joined the whaling trade as *La Liberte*. Declared unseaworthy after an accident in the 1790s, she was condemned at Newport, Rhode Island.

---

2.   W Falconer, *A Universal Dictionary of the Marine* (London 1780, reprint London 1970).

TABLE 1: **Specifications**

Burthen (tons)	366^{49}⁄₉₄
	(*ft-ins*)
Length on lower deck	97-8
Keel	81-0
Breadth (max)	29-2
Depth in hold	11-4

As mentioned above, numerous new details of *Endeavour* have come to light, making separate treatment of hull and rigging necessary.

Hull

Stern. A decorated stern on *Endeavour* models has only been accepted since the 1960s. Previously she was believed to have had no stern decoration at all, as in W A Falconer's bark[2] description. Although F H af Chapman showed ornamental sterns on nearly all his bark draughts, model makers and painters did no more than to put the ship's name on the upper counter of the stern. It was only after Sydney Parkinson's sketches became more widely know that painted or carved stern decoration began to appear frequently. Although the undefined nature of Parkinson's sketch means that the exact details of *Endeavour*'s decoration will remain a matter of contention, what is clear is the absence of the ship's name from the upper counter. Since the Royal Navy only adopted this previously French practice in 1772, four years after *Endeavour* sailed on her voyage of exploration, it is more than likely that the painted name never existed.

It has been claimed that the stern drawing on draught No. 3814c (which combines the sheer plan, body lines, stern and deck plans, and also gives the Woolwich masts and spars measurements) is a nineteenth-century concoction, as it is drawn on draughting linen, a nineteenth-century material. Whatever the reasons for a later redrawing of the draught (possibly preservation), taking the measurements from the other two, undisputed, draughts shows that the stern will shape similarly to that indicated on the redrawn draught. Furthermore, it also shows a taffrail cove above the windows, fashionable on British ships of the later eighteenth century, the sort of detail that a draughtsman of the nineteenth century would be unlikely to include in a draught he was inventing. This stern drawing should therefore be taken seriously. It can easily be proved that this draught and Parkinson's sketch of the stern do not conflict with each other by converting a three-quarter stern view photograph of an appropriately-decorated model into a sketch similar to Parkinson's view.

Besides showing ornamentation, Parkinson's sketch also finally lays to rest the false assertion that the *Endeavour* had five stern windows, a myth which has haunted all models and paintings of the ship. The central window was a dummy, added for purely aesthetic reasons. Arguments about the number of actual windows should never have arisen, since the size of the helmport in the lower counter and the quarterdeck shows that the rudder stock passed up through the cabin enclosed in a rudder-trunk, a solid wooden protective casing, which took up the whole space between the two centre counter-timbers and thus the space behind the so-called 'centre window' and no shipwright would give a window to a rudder-trunk. Its bogus nature is further confirmed by Parkinson's sketch, which shows shutters on only the outer four windows, the dummy centre window not having them as it did not need them. This is underlined by draughts of similar ships and by an interesting passage in Lieutenant William Bligh's log of the *Bounty* regarding the false centre window.[3]

Moving on to what one modern description of the *Endeavour* referred to as the 'strange hinged shutters', these were called 'dead-lights' and are shown on another of Parkinson's sketches covering the four outer windows. Evidence for the fitting of dead-lights to ships of this period can be found in Pierre Ozane's engraving of a French man-of-war in an Icelandic harbour c1780, showing open shutters, and the Admiralty draught of the *Bounty* dated 19 November 1787 indicating shutter lines above the stern windows. An entry in Bligh's log confirms the presence of these shutters.[4] Other written evidence is provided by E Bobrick[5] and W A Falconer[6], indicating that on smaller ships dead-lights were fitted like gun ports.

Parkinson's sketches have also settled the matter of the shape of the windows themselves, showing four round-topped windows set in rectangular frames (rectangular so that the hinged dead-lights could fit tightly). The false centre window has a larger semicircular section at the top as it is an arch between the inner mullions, rather than a real window in its frame.

Furthermore, the sketches prove that the *Endeavour* carried a stern lantern and that her rudder pendants were set up in a fashion mentioned by J R Röding in 1793 and defined by E Bobrick.[7]

Sheathing. It is confirmed by the early reports of the surveying yard officers and the subsequent instructions of the Navy Board that the *Endeavour* had a single bottom and that it was necessary to sheath and fill her in preparation for her voyage. Sheathing and filling at this time entailed paying the ship's bottom with a mixture of pitch, tar and sulphur (though some preferred paper and cow hair stuck on with tar) to prevent infestation with the marine worm *Teredo navalis* in tropical waters, and then 'sheathing' the hull below the waterline with a extra layer of thin fir planks. Further protection for the hull was provided by covering this outer layer with clout-headed filling spikes, hammered in ⅜ths of an inch apart.

Slight damage to the ship's sheathing was first mentioned by Robert Molyneux, the *Endeavour*'s Master, during their stay in Tahiti when he supervised the boot-topping of both sides of the ship. Cook described this process as 'careening' and used the term 'heaving down' when actual careening was considered. Heaving down was only undertaken during her stay at Batavia, whereas when the ship underwent emergency repairs after running aground on the Great Barrier Reef, she was just lightened forward as much as possible and her bows beached far enough so that the damage was accessible and an ordinary tide would not float her off, the procedure known as 'neaping'. On this occasion, as at Batavia, extreme loss of sheathing was reported by Cook in his log.[8]

Paying and painting. Study of the contemporary sources shows that the modern practice of painting the live work of *Endeavour* models and replicas white is incorrect. The ship's hull was payed with 'brown stuff' (a mixture of tar, pitch and sulphur) as protection against the worm, rather than with the more expensive 'white stuff' (train oil, resin and sulphur), a common practice in the Royal Navy of the eighteenth century. Both Cook[9] and Molyneux record boot-topping and careening using pitch and 'brimstone' (sulphur), both ingredients of 'brown stuff'.

Although 'white stuff' was not used on *Endeavour*, Cook did suggest in his journal the new procedure of painting boats' bottoms with white

3. R M Bowker, *Mutiny!! Aboard H.M. Armed Transport* Bounty *in 1789* (Old Bosham 1978) (reprint of Lt W Bligh's official log).
   'Dec. 27 1787. At ½ past 8 a Sea Struck us in the Stern and Stove it all to peices between the Cabbin Windows where the Sham Window is, which making a fair breach into the Cabbin it was with difficulty the Time Keeper & my Instruments were saved. One Azimh Compass was broke all to peices. Remarks: The Situation in the Morning was of a very serious Nature, but fortunately no sea Struck us while we were repairing the damage, which was owing to a want of firmness in the Joiners Work in the Middle part of the Stern opposite the Coating of the Rudder'.

4. Ibid. '24 Dec. 1787 A Sea struck us on the laboard Quarter and Stove the Dead light in and Shipt a great deal of Water, got another Dead light in and dryed the Ship'.

5. E Bobrik, *Handbuch der praktischen Seefahrtskunde* (Leipzig 1848, partial reprint Kassel 1978).
   'Whilst the rear cabin windows, mainly on merchantmen, are generally only opened in harbour, at sea they are closed with tight fitting port lids to protect against pounding waves from astern: there is a hatchway to be found on the cabin deck, through which the light comes in'.

6. W Falconer, *An Universal Dictionary of the Marine* (London 1780, reprint London 1970).
   'DEAD-LIGHTS, (*faux sabords*, Fr.) are strong wooden ports, made exactly to fit the cabin-windows, in which they are fixed on the approach of a storm, the glass-frames being taken out, which would otherwise be shattered by the surges, and suffer great quantities of water to pour into the ship.'

7. E Bobrik, *Handbuch der praktischen Seefahrtskunde* (Leipzig 1848, partial reprint Kassel 1978).
   'The rudder pendants are two ropes, each of them connected to a chain and hanging from an eye-bolt on each side of the after-piece's upper part, they lead over the taffarel to be fastened on deck. They are needed to hold the rudder, in case it gets unshipped by a heavy sea, and would be lost without these rudder pendants.'

8. J C Beaglehole ed., *The Journals of Captain James Cook, The Voyage of the* Endeavour *1768-1771* (Cambridge 1968).
   'This alone will be sufficient to let the worm into her bottom which may prove of bad consequence; however we must run all resk for I know of no method to remedy this but by heaving her down which would be a work of eminence labour & time, if not impractical in our present condition.'

9. Ibid. '. . . both paying them with Pitch and Brimstone, we found her bottom in good order and that the Worm had not got into it'.

lead, to protect them in 'Countrys where these worms are'. An Admiralty order of 6 October 1771,[10] only a few months after Cook's return, suggests his recommendation was acted upon.

No specific mention of a colour scheme for the hull's upper works can be found in the journals. The band of blue paint on the side planks below the quarterdeck was widely-accepted naval practice at this time but it cannot be confirmed for *Endeavour*. Wales were usually blackened with tar and the sides payed with varnish. Molyneux wrote on 5 July 1769 'Scrap'd the sides and pay'd them with varnish of Pine'. Masts, spars and deck furniture received the same coating

Airing and loading ports. Another area where misconceptions have abounded is the placement of the small loading and airing ports on both sides of the vessel. J H Röding describes airing ports thoroughly,[11] and if they were necessary on ordinary vessels, how much more essential would they have been on a collier, where the build-up of dust in the hold during loading or unloading would have threatened suffocation for the men below or even danger of an explosion, without good ventilation.

The number of airing ports fitted on models often does not match that shown on the draughts and they are frequently left without lids. In the case of the *Endeavour*, the as-purchased draught (3814b) shows five ports per side, whilst the last draught (3814c) shows nine. With one of the original ports shown planked over, five additional smaller ports can be seen. One port below the fore channels is not marked on the draught sheer plan (3814c) but it is shown on the lower deck plan in the carpenter's cabin. All these port were fitted with lids, as specified by Röding.[12]

The model presented to the Australian nation by Her Majesty The Queen in 1970 during the Australian bicentennial celebrations, which was built in the 1960s at the National Maritime Museum, Greenwich, has some of the larger loading and airing ports fitted with carriage guns. This was not a mistake made later by some misinformed restorer, as these wrongly-positioned guns are visible on photographs taken of the model when it was still at Greenwich. The position of these ports on the draughts, in the captain's bedchamber, the draughtsman's cabin and the forecastle, shows they were totally unsuited for the deployment of guns. None of *Endeavour*'s guns were mounted below decks.

Placement of guns. Endeavour sailed carrying ten 4-pounder carriage guns, six of which were mounted on the upper deck, the remainder being stored in the hold.[13] These four guns were brought up when the ship reached Tahiti, two being mounted on the quarterdeck and the others being sent ashore to arm Fort Venus,[14] and they were returned to the hold when she sailed. After the loss of the six guns on the upper deck after *Endeavour* struck the Great Barrier Reef, these four guns were brought out to replace them.[15] They were placed on the quarterdeck to assist in neaping the ship on the banks of the Endeavour River while repairs were made.

The ship was also equipped with twelve swivel guns, ten of which were mounted on swivel posts bolted to the outside of the quarterdeck

roughtree rails, and along the sides and in the bows. For details of the guns carried, see *Ordnance* p16.

Chess-trees and sheaves. All three draughts show that the *Earl of Pembroke/Endeavour* was fitted with chess-trees, pieces of wood fitted perpendicularly to the outboard with a hole in their upper part to lead the main course tacks inboard whilst extending their windward clew. Falconer reported the position of such chess-trees as being a main beam's length forward of the mainmast. The chess-trees on the *Earl of Pembroke* were probably not placed far forward enough to be adequate main tack fairleads for the rerigged *Endeavour* and for that reason a sheave fairlead was fitted during her refit between the timberheads almost abreast of the windlass. Further double sheave fairleads were fitted to the fore edge of the quarterdeck sheer break to accommodate the fore course and spritsail course sheets. Neither chess-trees nor fairleads appear on the Greenwich-built model, gunnel hooked blocks being used instead.

Channels. The ship's channels, or 'chain-wales', also underwent alteration during the Deptford refit. *Earl of Pembroke*'s fore channels originally contained five large and one smaller dead-eye, whilst the refitted *Endeavour*'s had seven large and one smaller. The foremost dead-eye was fitted approximately 2ft abaft the foremast on *Earl of Pembroke*, moving to a position abreast of the foremast's aft side after the refit.

The main channels on *Earl of Pembroke* were interrupted by one of the larger light-ports and were fitted with six plus one dead-eyes, the foremost of these again 2ft aft of the mast. As refitted, these channels ran above this light-port, with the same number and placement of dead-eyes as the fore channels. (See also under **Rig**.)

10. B Lavery, *The Ship of the Line, Vol.2* (London 1984).
    '. . . that the bottoms of all ship's boats of every kind to be painted in future with white lead instead of resin or any other composition.'

11. J H. Röding, *Allgemeines Wörterbuch der Marine* (Hamburg 1794, reprint Leiden 1969).
    '. . . especially is this the case in ships where the air is not only fouled by the constant perspiration and exhalation of men, animals and the often putrid bilge water, but also because of being a closed room without any circulation. It is an established fact that bad air, resulting from perspiration, is lighter than clean air. Therefore, such will always rise and swim above the latter like oil on water. One can easily convince oneself of that in a sick bay, as higher as one goes up in it, more irritable the smell becomes. Hence for attaining fresh air, it is apparent how very necessary the fitting of ports is, which are cut into the sides of a ship closely below the deck. Or, what would be better still, some higher up and others below to drive through the upper ones the bad air out.'

12. Ibid. '. . . the loading ports and light ports merchantmen have in their sides, are tightly caulked during a voyage.

13. J C Beaglehole ed., *The Journals of Captain James Cook, The Voyage of the* Endeavour *1768-1771* (Cambridge 1968).
    'Thursday 18th. (August 1768) Little wind and Clowdy. Struck down 4 guns in the hold, received on board 4 more with 12 Barrels of Powder and several other stores.'

14. Ibid. 'Saturday 29 April 1769 This Day got the four Guns out of the Hold and mounted 2 of them on the Quarter Deck, and the other 2 in the Fort on the bank of the River.'

15. Ibid. '. . . Tuesday 19 June 1770 In the AM got the 4 remaining guns out of the hold and Mounted them on the quarter deck.'

Anchor lining and naval-hood. The anchor lining was an extra layer of thin planks covering the side planking above the wales in the bows, to protect this area from damage from the bow anchor's flukes when it was catted or fished in order to be stowed. As this lining is not specifically marked on the draughts, its presence can only be assumed.

The 'naval-hood', another lining of soft wood enclosing the two hawse holes by the stem, can be identified in Parkinson's sketch of the bows. This method of protection for the hawse-holes, common practice on British-built ships of the period, is in contrast to the Continental method, where a rounded softwood bolster was placed below the holes.

Gammoning. Neither the draughts nor Parkinson's sketches give any details of *Endeavour*'s gammoning. However, a note in the log written by Master's Mate Pickergill[16] on a breezy day a few days before arrival in Rio de Janeiro not only confirms the presence of a gammoning ring, but also suggests the existence of a back-up gammoning, since the breaking of one of the bowsprit's main connections with the ship, whilst under sail on a breezy day, would have caused the headsails to wreak havoc with the whole rigging had they not been secured by a back-up gammoning. A disaster of these proportions, had it occurred, would surely have received more mention in the log than Pickergill's brief note. Therefore we can deduce that there was a gammoning ring bolted to *Endeavour*'s stem facing, and probably either an oblong hole cut into the stem head, or a second ring bolted to it, for a second gammoning, which practice accords with that shown on Chapman's draughts of larger barks.

Fittings

As with the fixed outboard features described above, the following descriptions of deck furniture and other fittings will proceed in order of their position on deck, starting just inside the taffrail.

Ensign staff. The presence of an ensign staff may safely be assumed despite its not being indicated on the draughts. Standing in a step between the taffrail and the rear of the helmport, it was further secured to the taffrail with an iron bracket. Its height above the taffrail was commonly one-third of the height of the mainmast.

Iron horse and flag lockers. Likewise a short iron horse for the mizzen sheet block can be assumed to have been aft of the helmport and flag lockers positioned just inside the taffrail.

Platform over the tiller. This was built during the rush of late refitting at Plymouth before the *Endeavour* sailed and is recorded in Cook's journal on 17 August 1768. The position of this platform has frequently been incorrectly described, for example by Beaglehole who claimed that Parkinson's stern view showed this platform. In fact what Parkinson drew was an awning over the cabin section of the quarterdeck. The most probable place for such a platform would have been at the helm (rudder) end of the tiller where its arc of movement was smallest, allowing easy access from port to starboard. Such bridges over long open tillers were not uncommon.

Steering wheel. This stood between the mizzen mast and the skylight, connected to the iron bracket of the tiller head (which was bent upwards to pass over the cabin fireplace flue) by the tiller rope, an untarred rope leading from the tiller head through a series of four blocks to turn five times around the barrel of the steering wheel (the centre turn being nailed to it to prevent slippage) and then back via a similar series of blocks to the tiller.

Binnacle. Although the existance of a binnacle aboard *Endeavour* is confirmed by an incident recorded in the log where a Maori was caught stealing the half-hour glass 'out of the Bitticle', there is no direct evidence for either its position or its appearance, which must therefore be deduced from general knowledge of eighteenth-century nautical practice. The common binnacle of the period was as described by Falconer, 'a wooden case or box, which contains the compasses, log-glasses, watch-glasses, and lights to shew the compass at night'. It consisted of three compartments, the lantern in the centre and the two compasses either side. It was necessary to have the two compasses at least 7ft apart to prevent reciprocal interference. The single compass binnacle was unknown at this time, being a nineteenth-century innovation not recorded before 1810.

The binnacle was usually placed directly in front of the steering wheel, so that the compasses could be read easily by the helmsman on one side and the officer of the watch on the other. Since the space forward of the wheel on *Endeavour* was taken up by the 4ft-wide skylight, the only viable position for the binnacle was beside and across the after portion of that light, the two compass compartments either side and the lantern in a bridging compartment between them over the skylight.

Skylight. Next in line was the skylight. The draughts show head-ledges and coamings 18in high, twice that of the main hatchway. Modern models often have a low inlaid grating covering this opening, which is incorrect. Contemporary literature and models are very specific that the only covering for a skylight of this sort was a glazed box hatch with protective iron bars. Since at sea the light ports were closed and caulked and the stern and badge windows covered with dead-lights, this skylight was the only source of daylight for the cabin and gratings would have defeated the object.

Capstan. The ship had a single capstan with its shaft rotating in a step on the cabin deck below. The capstan was not moved during the refit, and the newly-fitted companionway afore it and the skylight aft of it interfered somewhat with its easy operation, as the men on the bars now had

---

16. J C Beaglehole ed., *The Journals of Captain James Cook, The Voyage of the* Endeavour *1768-1771* (Cambridge 1968). '. . . found ye bolt for Gammoning the Bowsprit broke'.

to step aside when the bars passed over these obstacles. Principally used for handling heavy cargo, for warping or, as W Hutchinson wrote (1794), 'when it blows so strong that all hands cannot haul aft the fore sheet, but are obliged to heave it aft by the capstern . . .', the real test of its usefulness came during the desperate hours spent on the reef off northern Queensland.[17]

Companionway. The *Endeavour*'s companionway was almost certainly fitted with a protective 'companion',[18] to prevent the cabins below being swamped in bad weather. Open stairways, frequently fitted to models, were only found on larger ships where access to the officers' accommodation was below the quarterdeck and the ladderway lead on to the upper deck. Any water washing down that way would have run out through the scuppers on the main deck. This could not have happened on flush-decked ships or ships with a direct stairway from the quarterdeck to the cabins below, and all such ships, whether naval or merchant, had a protected companionway, as numerous contemporary models and paintings show. The companionway on *Endeavour* was the only access to the cabins and as such needed to be usable in all weathers without the risk of swamping them. There are several examples in the journals of the quarterdeck being awash, such as when Mr Green's astronomical observations taken in the Le Maire Strait on 14 January 1769 were felt to be inaccurate because 'when these observations were made, yet the sea ran so high that it filled the quarter deck three times while they were observing.'

Pumps. The absence of pumps from the Greenwich-built model of *Endeavour* is a major omission, if nothing else because of their vital role in saving the ship and thus the expedition after she struck the reef. The draft of the original *Earl of Pembroke* (3814b) shows two pumps abaft the mainmast, while the later *Endeavour* draught (3814a) shows four, two abreast the mainmast and two astern of this position. The presence of these four pumps is confirmed in the journals in Cook's report of the accident[19] and later in the repairs at Batavia.[20]

Bitts and gallows. The original draught of the *Earl of Pembroke* showed only topsail sheet bitts for the fore and mainmasts. Jeer bitts were added to the rear of both masts during the Deptford refit. It was here also that the spar gallows aft of the quarterdeck bulkhead and in the fore hatchway were fitted. These carried the reserve spars and booms etc, and the two smaller boats.

Hatchways, scuttles and other manholes. The coverings fitted to hatchways etc. are another 'grey area' in modelmaking, since they are not shown on the draughts. The common expedient of fitting all such openings on models with gratings is unsatisfactory. The basis for any approach to this issue must be that a hatchway's covering was determined by that hatchway's function.

The comments on the companionway above regarding the need to prevent swamping below decks apply equally to the main and fore hatchways. Covering the main hatchway with a grating provided excellent ventilation, but would have been wholly impractical on a ship of *Endeavour*'s size. Larger warships, with gun batteries below decks, needed the extra ventilation a grating provided when in action, but when rough seas prevented the lower deck guns being used, the gratings were tarpaulined and battened down to prevent flooding. *Endeavour*'s main hatch was therefore most probably covered by an inlaid hatch, tarpaulined and battened down at sea and only opened in harbour.

The fore hatch was the main access to the majority of the crew's quarters and therefore, like the companionway, had to be accessible in all weathers without risk of flooding. A watertight, strongly-hinged lid would therefore have been required, or better still something like the built-up entranceways for hatches on migrant ships. There is nothing in the sources to help with this matter, but general nautical literature of the period suggests that such a 'hood' was commonly used to cover not only the entrance to the cabins aft but also to the crew's quarters.[21] Therefore such a capping may be more realistic even than a hinged lid. A grating could only have been used for a small ventilation port, such as the one presumed to be over the galley, which would have been covered with a box hatch and battened down in bad weather.

Further forward, a scuttle on the port side gave access to the foremost fall, a space some 4ft in height below the forecastle, used as crew accommodation during the ship's days as a collier but unsuitable for *Endeavour*'s larger complement. This space could well have been used to house the ship's livestock (poultry, pigs and a goat, among others, being

17. J C Beaglehole ed., *The Journals of Captain James Cook, The Voyage of the* Endeavour *1768-1771* (Cambridge 1968). Cook: 'However I resolved to resk all and heave her off in case it was practical and accordingly turnd as many hands to the Capstan & windlass as could be spared from the Pumps and about 20' past 10 oClock the Ship floated and we hove her off into deep water having at this time 3 feet 9 inches water in the hold'.

18. W Falconer, *An Universal Dictionary of the Marine* (London 1780, reprint London 1970). 'COMPANION, a sort of wooden porch placed over the entrance or staircase of the master's cabin in a merchant ship.'

19. J C Beaglehole ed., *The Journals of Captain James Cook, The Voyage of the* Endeavour *1768-1771* (Cambridge 1968). 'By this time it was 5 oClock in the pm, the tide we observed now begun to rise and the leak increase upon us which obliged us to set the 3rd Pump to work as we should have done the 4th also but could not make it work. At 9 oClock the Ship righted and the Leak gained upon the Pumps considerably. This was an alarming and I may say terrible Circumstance and threatend immidiate destruction to us as soon as the Ship was afloat.'

20. Ibid. 'Carpenter's defect report on 10 October 1770 one Pump on the Larboard side useless the others decay'd within 1' Inch of the bore. an entry on 16 November 1770: Sent one of the decay'd Pumps up to Batavia to have a New one made by it.'

21. W Falconer, *An Universal Dictionary of the Marine* (London 1780, reprint London 1970). 'HOOD, a sort of low wooden porch, resembling the companion, and placed over the stair-case or ladder, which leads into the steerage or apartments, where the crew generally reside in a merchant-ship. The use of the hood is to admit the air and light, and at the same time prevent the rain from falling into the steerage.'
J H Röding, *Allgemeines Wörterbuch der Marine* (Hamburg 1794, reprint Leiden 1969). 'A capping can normally be found in top of the stairways to the cabin and to the crew quarters.'

mentioned). Again, given the need for constant access, a hinged, inlaid lid would have been fitted. Two doors in the rear bulkhead below gave further access to the foremost fall, and four ports in the bows, ahead of the fore channels, were for loading and ventilation.

During the restructuring of the quarterdeck at Deptford, a space 3ft wide was created athwart the main deck between the forward wall of the pantry and the quarterdeck bulkhead, which enclosed the mainmast, the rear gallows and the two forward pumps. No means of access to this space is shown on the draughts, but the need for access to all parts of the ship for maintenance purposes, as well as not to waste valuable storage space, suggests man-holes in the forward bulkhead, beside the short stairs to the quarterdeck (also not shown on the draughts).

Windlass. Endeavour's windlass stood aft of the 1ft-high step to the forecastle, right across the fore deck. Used for breaking anchors out of the seabed and other heavy heaving work beyond the capacity of the lighter capstan, it was mainly found on merchant ships and consisted of a horizontal shaft or 'barrel' between two bitt pins, sturdy oak posts with notches for the barrel trunnions to rotate in. A third post, the pawl bitt pin, stood in front of the middle of the barrel and prevented any reverse motion of the capstan when the anchor cable was under strain. Iron teeth, or 'pawls', engaged with the barrel, acting as a brake. The pawl bitt pin also supported the ship's belfry. On many models, and most recently the full-size replica of *Endeavour*, this arrangement has been shown as two pawl bitt pins with the belfry between them, but the draughts show the belfry supported by two uprights attached to a single pawl bitt pin, as shown in numerous lithographs dating from the early nineteenth century.[22]

Bowsprit step. The bowsprit step was part of the foremast topsail sheet bitts and consisted of a piece of timber, bolted above the bowsprit's squared heel to the bitt post. This was an arrangement common on barks, but a rather unsatisfactory one, as the constant strain of the headsail on the bowsprit must have had adverse results on the connections between the bitt post and the deck beams.[23]

Bumpkin fitting. Since bumpkins were needed for *Endeavour's* rigging and are shown in Parkinson's sketch of the bows, a timber was probably bolted aft of the stem on to the foremost deck beam for the iron heel brackets to house these booms extending over the bow. Bligh made reference to iron bumpkin brackets on the *Bounty* (see *Bumpkins* p21).

Anchors. The standard complement of anchors for a ship of c350 tons like *Endeavour* was three bower anchors, one stream anchor and one kedge anchor.[24] However, Cook's journal shows that several spare anchors were also carried. For example, during watering at Tierra del Fuego on 20 January 1769 it is recorded that the kedge anchor was lost, yet 18 months later Cook wrote of heaving taught upon *all five* anchors during the successful attempt to warp the ship off the Great Barrier Reef, in the course of which the small bower anchor was lost and the stream anchor only saved at the expense of its cable. Once the ship had been brought into Endeavour River for repairs, Cook reported that he 'Got a spare anchor and anchor stock a shore'. The fact that he refers to 'a', rather than 'the', spare anchor suggests that more than one was carried, especially given his later remark on 27 July 1770 that 'Carpenters [were] caulking the Ship and stocking one [!] of the spare anchors'. A spare anchor was the second largest carried aboard ship, after the sheet anchor, and was kept on the lower deck, only to be used in emergencies. Finally, 8 weeks after the reported loss of the small bower anchor, it is mentioned again, again suggesting the presence of a spare. Therefore, three spare anchors can be identified. Cook usually refers only to the best and small bower anchors, the stream anchor and the kedge anchor. Three mentions of a 'Costing anchor' probably refer to the sheet anchor, which in Falconer's words was what 'the seamen call their last hope, and never to be used but in great extremity'.

The sheet anchor was stowed furthest forward on the starboard side, with its cable on the port side to counterbalance it, with the small bower anchor identically arranged astern of it. The best bower anchor was stowed on the port side with the stream anchor, their cables to starboard. See Table 2 for the dimensions of the particular anchors.

TABLE 2: **Dimensions of Anchors**

Anchor	Weight (cwt)	Shank (ft-in)	Flukes (ft-in)
Sheet	21	13-2	4-5
Small bower	19	12-10	4-4
Stream	7½	9-3	3-1
Kedge	3½	7-3	2-5

The *Endeavour's* anchor cables were stored on the lower deck. Robert Molyneux, the ship's master, reported that in Tahiti, while he had the port side of the vessel boot-topped, he also had the small bower's cable stowed between decks, and while preparing the starboard side the best bower cable was stowed. A fortnight later he recorded the stowing of a new spare cable to the port side of the main hatchway.

Ordnance. The number and positioning of *Endeavour's* guns has already been dealt with. British 4-pounder carriage guns of the 1770s, of which

22. D R MacGregor, *Merchant Sailing Ships 1775 - 1815* (Watford, Hertfordshire 1980), (probably) J. R. Jobbins, A BRIG and AN INDIAMAN SHORTENING SAILS

23. J C Beaglehole ed., *The Journals of Captain James Cook, The Voyage of the Endeavour 1768-1771* (Cambridge 1968). 'Found the Bitts which Secure the foot of the Bow-sprit loose, this obliged us to put before the wind untill they were secured in the best manner our situation would admit.'

24. W Falconer, (Dr W Burney), *A New Universal Dictionary of the Marine* (London 1815, reprint United States 1970), Establishment and Value of Anchors for Ships of each Class in the British Navy, 1809.

ten were carried, were between 5ft 6in and 6ft long and weighed between 11 and 12cwt. They were mounted on carriages 3ft 2³⁄₁₆in long and 2ft 4¹¹⁄₁₆in wide across the axle trees.

Endeavour's twelve swivel guns of ½ or ¾lb calibre measured 2ft 10in long. The smallest type of naval artillery, they were loaded with langrage (loose shot) for short-range anti-personnel fighting. The guns' trunnions rested in an iron crotch or fork for elevation and depression and swivelled on vertical posts on the ship's sides. They could also be used to arm ship's boats, and Cook specifically requested four extra swivel guns to be fitted to the longboat as needed, which were supplied at Galleons Reach.

Boats. Endeavour sailed with five boats aboard, her official complement of a longboat, a pinnace and a yawl, as well as a skiff belonging to Joseph Banks[25] and another boat which was lost overboard in a gale on 1 September 1768.[26] The four remaining boats were sketched by Parkinson, who also preserved details of their rigs. That four boats remained is confirmed by Gunner Forwood's note on the Providential Channel incident (16 August 1770) reporting that 'Two boats were ahead sounding, the ship was being towed by the other two . . .'.

With regard to the positioning of the boats on board, the generally-assumed nesting above the reserve spars would only have been possible if the boats could have been fitted one inside the other. But the pinnace was at least as long as the longboat, although narrower, and the smaller yawl boat was wider than both of them, so the three official boats could not have been nested, and where would Banks' skiff, a narrow boat about as long as the pinnace, have gone?

Remarks by both Cook and Banks on 16 August 1770[27] not only confirm that the boats were not nested, but also tell us that the longboat was placed below the booms on deck, probably to port of the hatchways. Another short note by Cook on 27 August 1770[28] suggests that the two larger boats stood side by side. With the two larger boats sitting on the maindeck, and the yawl and skiff placed above the booms, each boat could be accessed separately, as Cook reported.

The largest boat carried, according to Cook's journal, was the longboat, not to be confused with the slightly different launch, which did not come into general use in the Royal Navy until 1780. This did not have a coating of white lead on its underside, as modellers often show. The longboat was only varnished and the result was that its bottom was destroyed by worms.[29] Although there is no direct evidence for the boat's length, her supposed position between the quarterdeck step and the fore hatchway would limit her to a maximum length of 19ft, a measurement in line with that for longboats on Royal Navy sloops of similar tonnage. Parkinson's sketches show that the longboat's rigs were a two-masted sliding gunter rig, with and without bowsprit and jib, a two-masted settee rig and a three-masted sprit rig with the foremast being square rigged.

The second boat carried was the pinnace. This type of boat was narrower than the longboat (a width to length ratio of 1:4 or 1:4.5 for a pinnace against 1:3 to 1:3.3 for a longboat), had a lower freeboard, a narrower stern and finer lines. They were usually a few feet longer than longboats, but the same restrictions on size would have applied to the pinnace (see above). The bottom was painted with white lead,[30] and she was rigged either with a two-masted sliding gunter rig or a single-masted sprit rig.

The smallest official boat carried was the yawl. The type is described by Falconer as being smaller than a cutter, but of similar shape and used for similar duties. As such, she was probably clinker-built and, as a utility craft, relatively wide and deep, with a width to length ratio ranging from 1:2.2 to 1:3.5. It is possible that *Endeavour*'s yawl was carvel-built, as an Admiralty order of 18 July 1769 stated that for ships on foreign service carvel-built yawls would be better as they were more durable and easier to repair. Parkinson's sketch of the yawl shows her with a single-masted sprit rig.

Of the two unofficial boats carried, the small boat belonging to the boatswain only appears in Cook's log when its loss in a gale is reported, and nothing else is known of it. Joseph Banks' skiff, however, is frequently mentioned. she first appears in Banks' account of the loss of the longboat 'which [. . .] broke adrift carrying with her my small boat which was made fast to her' at Rio (20 November 1769). Cook described this boat as a lighterman's skiff in his journal entry of 1 February 1769 and a month later it is reported that they 'lowerd down the Skift Mr. Banks went a Shooting in Her . . .' With the boat established as a skiff, which in general terms was a light rowing boat, a more specific description must be established. Falconer, a contemporary of Cook, described a skiff as 'a small boat resembling a yawl, also a wherry without masts or sails, usually employed to pass the river'. Parkinson's rough sketch appears to show a wherry-type boat, and together with Chapman's[31] drawing of

---

25. J C Beaglehole ed., *The Journals of Captain James Cook, The Voyage of the* Endeavour *1768-1771* (Cambridge 1968).
    'The weather was such as to admit Mr. Banks to row round the Ship in a Lighterman's skiff shooting birds.'

26. Ibid. 'Washed over board a small boat belonging to the Boatswain'.

27. Ibid. . . .'the Pinnace was under a repair and could not immediately be hoisted out, the Yawl was put into the water and the Long-boat hoisted out.' (Cook)
    'not merely was the pinnace under repair but the longboat under the Booms was lashd & fastned so well from our supposed security that she was not yet got out.' (Banks).

28. Ibid. '. . . and hoisted in the Pinnace and Long-boat up along side'.

29. Ibid. '. . . Friday 26th May 1769. This morning we haled the Pinnace a Shore to examine her bottom and had the satisfaction to find that not one worm had touched it, notwithstanding she hath been in the water nearly as long as the Long-boat; this must be owing to the white Lead with which her bottom is painted, the Long-boat being pay'd with Varnish of Pine, for no other reason can be assignd why the one should be preserv'd and the other distroyd, when they are both built on the same sort of wood and have been in equall use. From this circumstance alone the bottoms of all Boats send into Countrys where these Worms are ought to be painted with white lead, and the Ship supply'd with a good Stock in order to give them a new coat whenever its necessary, by this means they would be preserve'd free from these distructive vermin.'

30. Supra note 29.

31. F H af Chapman, *Architectura Navalis Mercatoria* (Stockholm 1768, reprint Rostock 1968), Plate L./9.

such a wherry, a picture of Bank's boat begins to emerge. The single square sail rig shown on Parkinson's sketch was probably only rigged for pleasure sailing in sheltered Tahitian waters.

Sweeps. Chance remarks in reports of perilous situations are often the only source of certain finer details of the ship, for example that long sweeps were part of the ship's equipment, mentioned by Cook during the Providential Channel incident.[32] These sweeps, about 28ft long, were used to move the ship when becalmed or in dangerous circumstances.

Accommodation. The captain, Mr Banks and his retinue of gentlemen had the use of the cabin deck. Only accessible through the quarterdeck companionway, it consisted of the great cabin, the lobby, the after fall with its skylight, the ladderway and cabins for the captain, Mr Banks, Mr Green and the draughtsmen, as well as the pantry, which had further storage space on either side of the pump well. The foremost doors on either side lead to the cabins of the latter, the aftermost were for the captain's and Banks' cabins respectively, while the second on the port side was for the third draughtsman's cabin and on the starboard side for Mr Green's cabin.

The only other storage and accommodation space other than the cabin deck aboard *Earl of Pembroke* had been the foremost fall (see above). During the Deptford refit, a new complete lower deck was added to the ship to accommodate the additional crew and supernumeraries for her scientific voyage. This deck was built 7ft below the main deck beams, which meant that the quarterdeck and forecastle encroached on its height for two-thirds of its length, leading to the highly unsatisfactory situation of a height of just 4ft for all the officers' and warrant officers' quarters and half the crews' quarters. It was only possible for men to stand upright in an area from the mainmast forward to the cook's oven. Given that this area was also used for the storage of anchor cables, spare anchors and sometimes even to accommodate livestock, living conditions below decks must have been far from comfortable.

Space for the boatswain, the carpenter and for a sail room was partitioned off in the bows, with a second sail room immediately forward of the foremast, leaving a passage on the port side to the gunner's store, the foremost space. Some steps lead down to the magazine.

Oven. The ship's oven stood forward of the fore hatch staircase, just outside the carpenter's and boatswain's cabins. Its position and the space left for it are marked on the draughts, giving it a size roughly 4ft by 4¼ft, which are the dimensions for the oven of a 20-gun ship which was equivalent to *Endeavour* in both tonnage and complement. The oven is specifically referred to by both Molyneaux and Cook[33] as being made of copper, whilst the usual material for the navy's new standard firehearth was iron.

Hold arrangement. The foremost section of the hold, reached through the gunner's store, was taken up by the ship's magazine, consisting of the

powder room and the adjacent light room. The enclosure around the mainmast, the well, prevented accidental damage to the pumps. Forward of the pump well was the shot locker, a storage space for the 4-pounders' round shot.

Entry to the general storage hold was through the fore, main and after hatchways, with the after hatch being situated below the cabin deck. To the rear of the latter a ladderway led down to the steward's room, the captain's store room and the slops storage. Below the steward's room was the fish room. Two scuttles aft of the mizzen mast gave access to the bread room at the rear of the steward's room.

Rig

Possible rig of the Earl of Pembroke. The terms 'cat-built vessel' or 'cat-built bark' were repeatedly used in correspondence between the Admiralty and the Navy board during the purchase of the *Earl of Pembroke* and they have haunted writers on the subject ever since. Why 'cat-built', and what actually is a 'cat-built bark'? Alan Villiers (in *Captain Cook, the Seamen's Seaman*) described the ship as 'a sort of ship-rigged cat'. This description may have served for a cat-built and bark-rigged vessel, but *Endeavour* was definitely not cat-built, as a comparison of the hull features of the two types shows.

First, the wing transom of a bark was always nearly straight and ship-like, resulting in a concave lower counter, as on *Endeavour*. In contrast, a cat's stern was much more rounded, lacking a lower counter and narrower than that of a bark. Second, the cabins and other accommodation on a cat extended above the level of the main deck, giving it a distinctive built-up forecastle and quarterdeck, sometimes even with a coach, and a deep and ship-like waist. A bark's accommodation was all below the level of the main deck or no more than half its height above it, and so they were commonly flush-decked. What passed for forecastle and quarterdeck on a bark was often no more than a low step in the deck fore and aft, which is clearly the case with *Endeavour*. Third, since on a bark the main deck was level with the tops of the frame timbers, no solid waist existed, an open roughtree rail surrounding the main deck.

All these features show that the *Earl of Pembroke*'s hull was not cat-built. Why then was she ever described as a 'cat-built bark'? Some clues to this problem may be found in the earliest draught (3814b) and in the purchase price of the ship, which suggest that the *Earl of Pembroke* was a 'cat-*rigged* bark' rather than the Admiralty's 'cat-*built* bark'.

The positioning of the foremost dead-eye in the fore and main channels (see *Channels* p13) on the draught of *Earl of Pembroke* indicates

32. J C Beaglehole ed., *The Journals of Captain James Cook, The Voyage of the* Endeavour *1768-1771* (Cambridge 1968).
'. . . the Yawl was put into the water and the Long- boat hoisted out and both sent ahead to tow which together with the help of our sweeps abaft got the Ships head round to the northward which seem'd to be the only way to keep her off the reef or at least to delay time.'

33. Ibid. 'Got the Copper Oven ashore and fix'd it in the Bank of the breast works.'

wider and lower courses than on the refitted *Endeavour*. A short-masted cat-rigged vessel with such sails would have required the foremost shroud placed further abaft the mast than the higher and smaller courses of a taunt-masted bark, to give the yards a similar degree of turning. One of F H af Chapman's draughts[34] shows identical placing (though smaller numbers) of dead-eyes on a smaller cat-rigged vessel. This draught of a polacre (kray) rigged small bark provides us with a comparable situation to the *Earl of Pembroke* dead-eye layout, also suggesting that the ship may have been fitted with pole masts.

Furthermore, the low valuation of the *Earl of Pembroke*'s masts and spars suggests these were the pole masts and yards of a light cat rig, worth no more than £56 17s 10d to the Navy as second-hand timber, compared with the full refit cost of £1357 17s 11d. A lighter rig such as this, associated with cats, could be worked by a smaller crew, an important economic concern in merchant ships, particularly colliers, as Hutchinson states.[35] Both sources, therefore, point to the *Earl of Pembroke* as originally purchased being a cat-rigged bark, her bark hull being described as such by the Deptford yard officers and later in her official registration.

The set-up of the dead-eyes on *Endeavour* provides the basis for the analysis of the ship's new rig. Comparable draughts by F H af Chapman[36] for a cat of 340 tons and a bark of 416 tons (both ship rigged) dated 1768 shows five fore and six main shroud pairs, whilst data from Steel[37] gives six fore and six main pairs on a sixth rate of 300-400 tons, five and five on a merchantman of 330 tons and six and six on one of 544 tons. With *Endeavour*'s eight dead-eyes on both fore and main channels, Steel's naval rig for ships of 350-400 tons, with six fore and six main shroud pairs and two standing backstay pairs, can be considered relevant for *Endeavour*. Cook's journal confirms the presence of the two backstays, reporting a sprung main topmast and both backstays broken on 22 June 1771.

Masts. The number of *Endeavour*'s sails has given rise to the conclusion that the rig was completed in all respects in accordance with navy rules. This was not entirely the case, as the mast dimensions on draught 3814c, taken on the ship's return from its historic voyage, show. It is arguable that these variations in spar dimensions show the hand of James Cook himself, a former merchant mariner and master's mate aboard a collier, rigging a tubby bark in what he knew from experience to be the best way. Cook may not have had any part in the selection of the vessel, but rigging of the *Endeavour* did not begin until he had taken command of her. Although there is no direct evidence that Cook influenced the rig of *Endeavour*, it is known that captains frequently did have some say in their rig, an entry in Lt William Bligh's log being one example.[38]

A comparison of the dimensions taken at Woolwich and the Royal Navy standard shows the taunt nature of *Endeavour*'s masts and the varying length of her spars. Most of these mast lengths were considerably longer than the standard laid down in 1711 by William Sutherland,[39] which was still relevant to Royal Navy ships at the end of the eighteenth century. See Table 3.

TABLE 3: **Comparison of Mast Dimensions**

Mast	*Endeavour* Woolwich Yard 16 Oct 1771		Royal Navy standard	
	Length (yds-ins)	Diameter (ins)	Length (yds-ins)	Diameter (ins)
Mainmast	23-4	21	21-5	18¾
Topmast	13-19	12	12-21	12
Topgallant to hounds	6-10			
Pole	3-3	6		
Foremast	21-26	19¾	18-28½	16½
Topmast	12-28	12	11-6½	11½
Topgallant to hounds	5-26			
Pole	2-27	5¾		
Mizzen mast	16-29	14⅙	18-4¼	12½
Topmast	8-10		9	8⅜
Pole	3-26	8		
Bowsprit	11-12	19⅛	12-24½	18¾
Jib boom	11-15	9⅞	9-2	7⅞

Therefore, *Endeavour*'s mainmast was 5ft 11in taller than the Navy standard, her topmast 8ft 10in taller, and her mizzen mast apparently some 6ft shorter, if we accept the common interpretation of the measurements given. The topmasts and topgallants also followed this trend, as shown in Table 3.

The inconsistency of the disproportionately short mizzen mast is a feature of all modern reconstructions of the *Endeavour* and is based on two features of draught 3814c. First, the length of the mizzen mast is given as 16yds 29in and, second, the draught clearly shows the mast to have been stepped in the hold. Thus the models etc. have this shorter mizzen mast. Although it is certainly the case that the mast stepped in

34. F H af Chapman, *Architectura Navalis Mercatoria* (Stockholm 1768, reprint Rostock 1968), Plate XXIX/8.

35. W Hutchinson, *A Treatise on Naval Architecture* (Liverpool 1794, reprint London 1969). '. . . are in the colliers bound to London, where many great ships are constantly employed, and where wages are paid by the voyage, so that interest makes them dexterous and industrious to manage their ships with few men,[. . .] more so than perhaps in any other trade by sea in the world. [. . .] that these ships being adapted for this trade, are rigged as light as possible.'

36. F H af Chapman, *Architectura Navalis Mercatoria* (Stockholm 1768, reprint Rostock 1968), Plates XIX/26 and XXIV/35

37. D Steel, *Elements of Mastmaking, Sailmaking and Rigging* (London 1794, reprint New York 1932).

38. R M Bowker, *Mutiny!! Aboard H.M. Armed Transport* Bounty *in 1789* (Old Bosham 1978) (reprint of Lt W Bligh's official log). '. . . on the 4th September from an application I had made the Lower Masts were got out and Shortned and the Lower and Topsail Yards were cut on shore agreeable to my request.'

39. W Sutherland, *The Ship-builders Assistant* (London 1711, reprint Rotherfield 1989). 'It was the Opinion of a very good Mast-maker, to take the Length of the Lower Gundeck, and the extream Breadth, and adding them together, to take 'that for the Length of the Main-mast in Feet.'

the hold, the height given is probably that for a mast stepped on the lower deck. No contemporary source supports the stepping of a mast of this length in the hold, and it is highly unlikely that an experienced seaman like James Cook would have accepted a ship where the important aft steering sail was 9ft shorter than usual.

No contemporary pictures of the ship show this short mizzen mast. Thomas Luny's 1781 painting of a collier identified as the *Earl of Pembroke*[40] shows a normal-sized mizzen, as does the one eye-witness representation of *Endeavour*'s rig, *The Endeavour at Sea* by Parkinson, as do the engravings made from his sketches, (1) *The Endeavour repaired in Endeavour River*, (2) *A View of the great Peak & the adjacent Country, on the West Coast of New Zealand*, (3) *A View of an Arched Rock, on the Coast of New Zealand, with an Hippa, or Place of Retreat, on the Top of it* and (4) *Matavai Bay, Tahiti*.[41] All of these have the *Endeavour* as a background feature and none shows a short mizzen mast.

As this evidence points to a different mizzen mast length than that in accepted reconstruction practice, a cross-reference to general eighteenth-century nautical practice seems appropriate. Throughout the century, the commonly-accepted formula for the length of a mizzen mast was 6/7ths of the length of the mainmast. John Davis[42] gave for taunt masts 'The Mizon Mast if it steps in the Hold 2⅓ of the Beam; but if it steps on the Gun-deck twice the Beam' and J H Röding wrote in 1794 of normal mizzen mast length being 1¾ times the beam. If all these measurements are plotted on a drawing, they result in an outcome approved by F H af Chapman, who wrote in 1768 that the correct height for the mizzen mast was level with the mainmast top. The *Endeavour*, if the length of its mainmast is taken as 16yds 29in stepped in the hold, is the only divergence from these rules. However, if the mast is stepped on the lower deck (which, admittedly, there is no indication of on the draughts) it conforms to the rigging rules of the day. Using the 6/7ths of mainmast rule, it is longer than the Naval standard by 1ft 8in.

However, it is almost certain that the draught is correct in showing the mast stepped in the hold. But the discrepancy can be explained as a draughtsman's error in copying the surveyor's notes onto the draught, since using the 6/7ths of mainmast rule the length of the mast would have been 19yds 29in, this length giving a mast of the correct proportions. It is easy to see how such a mistake could have occurred.

A further example is the *Adventure* (ex-*Marquis of Rockingham*), the smaller ship on Cook's second circumnavigation. Built in 1770 in the same shipyard and to a very similar design to that of the *Endeavour*, she was of similar dimensions, but with a mizzen mast length of 19yds 12in, close to the assumed 19yds 29in for *Endeavour* and again indicating larger masts than those laid down by the Navy.

Another means of determining the length of the mizzen mast is to take the common rule whereby the topmast was ⅗ths the length of the mizzen, the combined measurements of the topmast and pole of 12yds would give a mizzen mast length within 7in of the 19yds 29in measure. As the measurements stand, the mizzen would be too short and the topmast too long, begging the question why important steering sail volume would have been sacrificed to enlarge another driving sail. The argument presented above brings the masts into the correct proportion and agrees with the only eye-witness sketch and common sense.

Spars. Likewise, *Endeavour*'s spar measurements differed from the Naval rules of the period. Table 4 compares the measurements taken at Woolwich in 1771 with rules and dimensions taken from three eighteenth-century sources, Sutherland, Falconer and Steel, dated 1711, 1769 and 1794 respectively.[43]

TABLE 4: **Comparative Spar Dimensions**

Spar	Rule	Dimension (ft-in)
Main yard		
Sutherland	7/8 x mainmast	55-6
Falconer	(RN rule c1770)	
	0.561 x gundeck	54-10
Steel	8/9 x mainmast	56-4
Endeavour		**47-10**
Fore yard		
Sutherland	7/8 x main yard	48-6
Falconer	0.874 x main yard	48-0
Steel	7/8 x main yard	49-3
Endeavour		**44-2**
Crossjack yard		
Sutherland	slightly longer than main topsail yard	c 31-0
Falconer	as fore topsail yard	37-10
Steel	as fore topsail yard	34-9
Endeavour		**39-14 or 40-2**
Main topsail yard		
Sutherland	5/9 x main yard	30-10
Falconer	0.726 x main yard	39-9
Steel	5/7 x main yard	39-8
Endeavour		**39-10**
Fore topsail yard		
Sutherland	5/9 x main yard	30-10
Falconer	0.715 x fore yard	34-4
Steel	7/8 x main topsail yard	34-9
Endeavour		**36-1**

40. Thomas Luny, 'The *Earl of Pembroke* leaving Whitby Harbour', National Library, Canberra A.C.T.

41. (1) & (4) R & T Rienits, *The Voyages of Captain Cook* (London 1968); (2) & (3) S Parkinson, *Journal of a Voyage to the South Seas in HMS* Endeavour (London 1784, reprint London 1984).

42. J Davis, *The Seaman's Speculum* (London 1711, reprint N. R. G. 1985).

43. W Sutherland, *The Ship-builder's Assistant* (London 1711, reprint Rotherfield 1989); W Falconer, *An Universal Dictionary of the Marine* (London 1780, reprint London 1970); D Steel, *Elements of Mastmaking, Sailmaking and Rigging* (London 1794, repr. New York 1932).

Mizzen topsail yard

Sutherland	½ x fore yard	24-3
Falconer	0.75 x fore topsail yard	25-9
Steel	⅔ x main topsail yard	26-3
Endeavour		**32-1**

Main topgallant yard

Sutherland	½ x topsail yard	15-5
Falconer	0.69 x main topsail yard	27-5
Steel	⅗ x main topsail yard	23-9
Endeavour		**31-8**

Fore topgallant yard

Sutherland	½ x topsail yard	15-5
Falconer	0.69 x fore topsail yard	23-8
Steel	⅗ x fore topsail yard	20-10
Endeavour		**28-9**

Spritsail yard

Sutherland	5/7 x fore yard	34-8
Falconer	as fore topsail yard	34-4
Steel	as fore topsail yard	34-9
Endeavour		**38-9**

Sprit topsail yard

Sutherland	½ x spritsail yard	17-4
Falconer	as fore topgallant yard	23-8
Steel	as fore topgallant yard	28-10
Endeavour		**31-8**

Apart for the lower yards, which were several feet shorter than the range of eighteenth-century examples given in Table 4, all the other yards were made for larger than normal sails. The picture which emerges, therefore, is of an English bark rig with a mizzen topsail. Although the absence of a mizzen topsail would become one of the main differentiating features of a bark rig in the nineteenth century, in this period it was far less common. It was referred to by Falconer in 1769 ('however peculiarly appropriated by seamen to those which carry three masts without a mizzen topsail . . .') but only as an abnormality (hence 'peculiarly'), and Falconer did not consider it worthwhile providing a illustration of such a bark rig, although all other dominant rigs were represented. Furthermore, it was not mentioned either by Chapman in 1769, who described larger barks as ship rigged, nor by Röding in 1794, who wrote that barks carried a frigate rig, and few eighteenth-century pictures exist of such a rig, one of the earliest being by E Gwyn in 1780.[44] Features of a bark rig of this period were the long and narrow courses, which did not overlap each other, and the definitive long masts and short yards with flying topgallant sails, as described by Hutchinson.[45]

Bumpkins. One item of rigging which appears on none of the reconstructions of *Endeavour*, yet is clearly shown on Parkinson's sketches as a pair of booms extending obliquely forward from the bows, is the bumpkins. When questioned about their absence from the cutaway model on display at Greenwich, the builder R Lightley wrote that he did not know what Parkinson's sketch was supposed to represent and was not prepared to guess.[46] As Parkinson clearly showed these booms in his sketch, it is necessary to look for further evidence of their presence or absence.

Reference to Chapman, Röding, Lever,[47] Hutchinson *et al.* provides strong evidence for *Endeavour* being fitted with bumpkins. Many of the illustrations in Röding, taken from Lescallier's work,[48] indicate downward-curving bumpkins which by no stretch of the imagination could be described as catheads. They can be seen on drawings of cats, galliots, snows and brigs. Although Chapman's ten bark draughts do not specifically show bumpkins, they do show extended hawse timbers, sometimes even notched out for bumpkin support. The fact that these booms are not shown on every plan Chapman left us does not necessarily mean that those ships were not fitted with them. For example, not all of his frigate draughts show bumpkins.

The argument that bark tacks were taken under the catheads (see footnote 46) is based on a passage in Lever[49] which refers to 'small vessels in the Merchant Service'. However, small merchant vessels were rigged in a variety of ways, many being fore and aft rigged, and if square rigged, the positions of their masts and cat-heads or the cut of their sails fre-

44. In D R MacGregor, *Merchant Sailing Ships 1775-1815* (Watford, Herts. 1980).

45. W Hutchinson, *A Treatise on Naval Architecture* (Liverpool 1794, repr. London 1969). 'The square sails, suitable to taunt masts and short yards, as here recommended, will be in proportion, deep and narrow, which will trim and stand much fairer upon the wind, than if they were shallow and broader; [. . .] To endeavour to make a ship sail by the wind, and turn well to windward, deserves the greatest regard, because safety, as well as many other great advantages depend upon it. The good effects of deep and narrow squaresails, cannot be better recommended as answering this purpose, than by the performance of ships in the coal and timber trades to London, though the designed properties in building and fitting these ships, are burden at a small draft of water, to take and bear the ground well, and to sail with few hands, and little ballast; yet these ships perform so well at sea, that government often makes choice of them for store ships, in the most distant naval expeditions; and in narrow channels among shoals; and in turning to windward, in narrow rivers, there are no ships of equal burden can match them, which I attribute a great deal to their deep narrow squaresails, [. . .] Where a deal of canvas is wanted, to sail fast large, the narrow deep square sails have in height what they want in breadth; and the flying sails, including the topgallant sails as such, being all of lighter canvas, may be made as large as things will admit of, to answer this purpose in little winds; and when it comes to blow so strong, that these flying sails cannot be carried, then the standing squaresails will be found broad enough.'

46. R Lightley, personal communication 14 November 1983. 'This was discussed with Jim Lees (Rigger of the Greenwich-built models and author of *The Masting and Rigging of English Ships of War 1625 to 1860*), the world authority in English rigging you will agree, and he said that there is no evidence that boomkins existed on Barks. Certainly Chapman's *Architectura Navalis Mercatoria* of 1768 does not show any in something like 10 examples. Lees believes that the tacks were taken under the catheads to opposite sides and belayed. What those curved lines on the bow sketch are (they are not repeated on the stern view) is anybody's guess. I am not prepared to guess.'

47. D Lever, *The Young Sea Officer's Sheet Anchor* (London 1819, repr. New York 1963).

48. A Lescallier, *Vocabulaire des Terms de Marin* (Paris 1777, repr. Grenoble 1968).

49. D Lever, *The Young Sea Officer's Sheet Anchor* (London 1819, repr. New York 1963). 'In small vessels in the Merchant Service, the Tack is often slack-laid with four Strands, and as they carry no Boomkin, the Tack is taken under the after side of the Cat-head and belayed to the Timber-head before it.'

quently varied from those of larger ships, and therefore a need for bumpkins did not always arise. It should also be noted that merchant ships often had two cloths on each side of the foresail gored toward the clew, therefore reducing the width from clew to clew by approximately 8ft. Small ships which occasionally hoisted a squaresail when running before the wind carried a squaresail boom for clew spreading, which performed the same function as bumpkins. Furthermore, when it is considered that larger ships of the mid-nineteenth century, which had their foremasts set further aft than ships of this period, also used their cat-heads for this purpose, it becomes clear that the fitting of bumpkins was determined by necessity, by the position of the foremast, the shape of the sail and the placing of the catheads. Hutchinson also commented on the necessity for bumpkins.[50] His advice on the windward clew position, gained from experience, could only have been followed on *Endeavour* with the bumpkins sketched by Parkinson, and certainly not by taking the fore tack under the cat-heads as in all existing reconstructions. The cat-heads were approximately one-third closer to the ship's longitudinal axis than the chess-trees, which served the same purpose for the main course, and by pulling the fore course's windward clew in instead of out, they would have exerted an opposite effect to that intended.

That bumpkins were fitted to other, similar Royal Navy vessels is shown by an entry in Bligh's log of the *Bounty*.[51] It could be argued that the *Bounty*, a typical bark, differed from *Endeavour* in that she was built with a head, and bumpkins were usually fastened to the bulkhead or knight-heads and main head rails of a ship. But *Bounty*'s head would not have been able to support bumpkins of the length required, and they therefore would have to have been fitted to the foredeck as on *Endeavour*, so as to project from each side of the bow to haul in the fore tack.

The need for the windward spreading of course clews with loose bumpkins had been stated as early as 1627 by Captain John Smith.[52] Two hundred years later Bobrick gave the ideal position for a bumpkin. The position of the bumpkin's inner end is found by drawing a line half a yard's length long at an angle of 36° from the centre of the mast. The bumpkin should run out at the same angle as the fully-braced yard to a length outside the centre line determined by the fore clew. The length of such a bumpkin would therefore be half the length of the fore yard minus the length of the yardarm, less another 18in.

Topgallant yards. Another feature of *Endeavour* that has not featured in any of the reconstructions is her 'flying' topgallant yards and sails. Frequent mentions in Cook's journal of bringing the topgallant yards down or rigging them across again and references to them as light sails can be taken together with Hutchinson's description of barks employed in the London coal and timber trades, in which he classified the topgallants as flying sails.[53]

These yards were lowered and hoisted with the help of large thimbles or 'travellers'. Fitted with a tail of about 3ft of rope, they ran in pairs up and down the backstays, with the tails fastened to the yardarms to stop them swinging with the ship's motion. 'Flying of sails' was defined by

Steel and Falconer as '. . . setting them in a loose manner; as royal sails without lifts, or sheets, the clues being lashed; as small topgallant-sails, jibs without stays; and as studding-sails without booms'. In this case, the sheets and braces could be untoggled and the light sling-parrel dismantled.

Flying jib. That *Endeavour* had a flying jib is show in an entry in the anonymous manuscript fragment for 28 October 1768,[54] where the loss of the jib traveller is reported. Since Cook himself did not even mention this incident, it can only have been a minor problem. A far greater problem (worthy of further mention) would have been a severed connection between the jib stay and the traveller, but the fact that the jib was simply hauled in and the traveller replaced and that there was no mention of a jib stay at all, strongly suggests that the ship carried a flying jib.

Studding sails. Three entries in Cook's journal for 23 December 1768, 31 January 1769 and 2 February 1769 point to the use of studding sails, and therefore the temporary rigging of lower and topmast studding sails can be assumed. Topgallant studding sails would not have been carried. The fitting of goose-necked swinging studdingsail booms to the mainmast is confirmed in literature dating from 1711, but there is no such evidence for a similar arrangement on the foremast before the last decade of the eighteenth century. Before that time the boat boom extended outboard between timberheads and was fastened on deck.

Two other entries on 16 February 1769[55] tell of the existence of a driver. At that time a driver was a squaresail hoisted to the gaff's peak and with its sheets fastened to a boom, pushed over and lashed to the lee rail.[56]

50. W Hutchinson, *A Treatise on Naval Architecture* (Liverpool 1794, repr. London 1969). 'The foretacks of all ships should be made to stand by bumpkins, or at the cat-heads, &c. as far to windward as the main tacks.'

51. R M Bowker, *Mutiny!! Aboard H.M. Armed Transport* Bounty *in 1789* (Old Bosham 1978) (reprint of Lt W Bligh's official log). 'Friday 28th Dec. 1787 5 am Set the Main Staysail. A Sea carried away the larboard Bumpkin and Iron Braces'.

52. Captain J Smith, *A Sea Grammar* ed. K Goell (London 1627, reprint London 1970). 'and boomes it out with a boome or long pole; which we use also sometimes to the clew of the maine saile, fore saile and spret saile when you goe before the wind, or quartering, else not'.

53. W Hutchinson, *A Treatise on Naval Architecture* (Liverpool 1794, repr. London 1969). 'Where a deal of canvas is wanted, to sail fast large, the narrow deep square sails have in height what they want in breadth; and the flying sails, including the topgallant sails as such, being all of lighter canvas, may be made as large as things will admit of, to answer this purpose in little winds; and when it comes to blow so strong, that these flying sails cannot be carried, then the standing squaresails will be found broad enough.'

54. J C Beaglehole ed., *The Journals of Captain James Cook, The Voyage of the* Endeavour *1768-1771* (Cambridge 1968). '. . . at 6 AM found the Traveller of the Jibb Gone - hauled him down & Got a new one.'

55. Ibid. '. . . and very heavy seas from the SSW, one of which brok upon the quarter and carried away the driver boom' (Cook); '. . . Shipt a Sea on the Labd Quarter wch broke the Lashings (and with the lee Rowl lost) the Driver Boom.' (Hicks).

56. K H Marquardt, *Eighteenth Century Rigs & Rigging* (Conway Maritime Press 1992), pp.103, 237.

Sources

ORIGINAL DRAUGHTS

No. 3814(b); undated, and headed 'The Draught of His Majesty's Bark *Endeavour*', it was produced soon after the *Earl of Pembroke* was purchased by the Navy on 28 March 1768. Proposed alterations are indicated with broken lines in red ink.

No. 3814(c); dated Deptford Yard 11 July 1768 and headed 'The Draught of His Majesty's Bark *Endeavour*, as fitted at this port, her body taken off in the single dock'.

No. 3814(a); dated 16 October 1771, and taken off for *Endeavour*'s conversion into a store ship.

No. 3819(a); 'Plans of His Majesty's Bark *Endeavour*, as fitted at Deptford in July 1768'. This sheet contains the deck plans (3814(c)).

ARTWORK BY SYDNEY PARKINSON

BL ADD 9345, fol. 16v: 'The *Endeavour* at Sea'.

BL ADD 9345, fol. 57: A three-quarter stern view.

BL ADD 9345, fol. 50: Bow view.

BL ADD 9345, fol. 21v & 22: Ship's boats.

BL ADD 23921, fol. 6a: 'One Tree Hill and Matavai Bay, Tahiti'.

'View of the Great Peak and the adjacent country, on the west coast of New Zealand' and 'View of an arched rock, on the coast of New Zealand, with a Hippa, or place of retreat, on the top of it', in Sydney Parkinson, *Journal of a Voyage to the South Seas in HMS* Endeavour, London 1784, repr. 1984.

'The Endeavour River with the ship being repaired': engraving after Sydney Parkinson.

PUBLISHED SOURCES

Beaglehole, J C, *The Journals of Captain James Cook Vol 1: The Voyage of the* Endeavour *1768-1771*, CUP for the Hakluyt Society, 1968

Parkinson, Sydney, *Journal of a Voyage to the South Seas in HMS* Endeavour, London 1784, repr. 1984

FURTHER READING

Barrow, J, *Captain Cook's Voyages of Discovery*, London 1906, repr. 1967

Bennett, S, *Australian Discovery and Colonisation*, Sydney 1865, repr. 1981

Library of New South Wales, *Bibliography of Captain James Cook*, Sydney 1970

Rienits, R and T, *The Voyages of Captain Cook*, London 1968

Roberts, L, *The* Endeavour, *Captain Cook's First Voyage to Australia*, London 1956

Villiers, A, *Captain Cook, the Seamen's Seaman*, London 1967

Captain James Cook, RN, FRS. Oil painting by Author 1983, after Nathaniel Dance, 1776.

Starboard bow view of a recent model of *Endeavour* built by Mr Alan Tyler of Frankston, Victoria. Originally built from a kit, this model has been heavily modified to show features from the author's research. (*Mr Alan Tyler*)

Larboard quarter of the Tyler model, showing some features from Parkinson's sketch. (*Mr Alan Tyler*)

Bow of the Tyler model with naval-hoods, bumpkins and anchor lining. (*Mr Alan Tyler*)

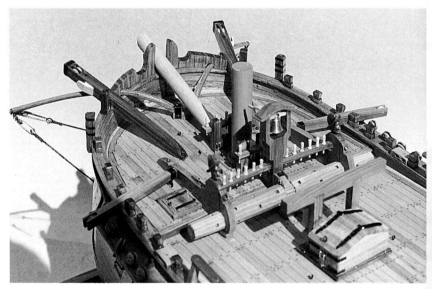

Stern of the Tyler model, clearly showing the decoration indicated by Parkinson, the dead-lights fitted to the four windows and a rudder pendant to starboard. (*Mr Alan Tyler*)

Fore deck of the Tyler model. Note the hood over the fore hatchway, the hinged fore fall hatch, the single pawl bitt with its belfry on the windlass, the belay rails between the bitts and the bumpkins. (*Mr Alan Tyler*)

Model built at the National Maritime Museum, Greenwich and presented to the Australian nation in 1970 by the Queen, kept in the Australian National Maritime Museum, Sydney. Note the airing ports without lids, missing bumpkins, the gratings on the hatchways, the nested boats, the white-painted hull and the gun in the fore fall light port. (*Photograph by Author*)

Below left:
Larboard midships view of the Greenwich-built model. Again note the guns in the lighting ports, the grating over the skylight, the open stairways and the absence of the gangway steps and the pumps. (*Photograph by Author*)

Below:
Starboard quarter of the Greenwich-built model, showing five windows, no stern roughtree rail and the rudder pendants leading across the counter. (*Photograph by Author*)

Starboard quarter view of a typical earlier model of *Endeavour*. Note the unadorned stern, the five small, rectangular windows, the name on the counter and the short mizzen mast, amongst other inaccuracies. (*Australian National Maritime Museum, Sydney*)

One of the six 4-pounder guns and some iron ballast jettisoned by *Endeavour* after striking the Great Barrier Reef, on display in the Australian National Maritime Museum, Sydney. (*Photograph by Author*)

Mock-up windlass aboard the Fremantle replica, showing double pawl bitts (only a single pawl bit on the draughts), and the ship's designer David White's head carved on the bitt pins. (*Mr William Haddock, Seaford, Victoria*)

Stern view of the Fremantle replica of *Endeavour*, one day before her launch. Her designer, David White, is standing on the left. The stern is of higher and narrower proportions than indicated on the draughts, being more like that of the Greenwich based, Lightley-built.model. The dead-lights are not recessed as Parkinson indicated, provision being made to hang these from eyebolts outside. There is also no taffrail cove above the windows. (*Mr William Haddock, Seaford, Victoria*)

Below:
Quarterdeck of the Fremantle replica the day before her launch, showing the wheel, skylight, capstan, companion stairway, bitts and pumps. The deck is covered with tarpaulins to protect it from damage. (*Mr William Haddock, Seaford, Victoria*)

View from the quarterdeck of the Fremantle replica during construction. Note the curved spar gallows, which is not identifiable on the draughts. (*Mr William Haddock, Seaford, Victoria*)

Quarterdeck of the Fremantle replica showing a small rudder house over the helmport rather than an upper helmport coat. Although not found in the draughts, it has been considered as a possibility for *Endeavour*. One is shown on the draughts of the *Bounty* and on a model of a French brig from 1805. (*Mr William Haddock, Seaford, Victoria*)

The Castlegate Quay Heritage Project's replica of *Endeavour* under construction. The hull is steel-built and at this stage all the exterior fittings have yet to be added. (*Castlegate Quay Heritage Project, Stockton-on-Tees*)

Stern view of the Castlegate Quay replica. She has five windows in her undecorated stern and here too the short mizzen mast can be seen. (*Castlegate Quay Heritage Project, Stockton-on-Tees*)

Sketch of the larboard quarter of *Endeavour*, showing stern details, by Sydney Parkinson, the expedition's draughtsman. This is a mine of information not found in the draughts or the journals, showing the stern decoration and the arrangement of the windows, the stern lantern, the rudder pendants and an awning over the great cabin. It also shows the hinged lids covering the airing ports etc., so often left off of models. The fact that all these ports are open suggests that the drawing was made during the ship's stay in Tahiti. (*British Library*)

32

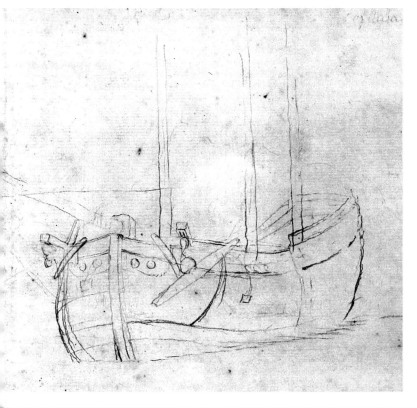

Above left:
Larboard bow sketch of *Endeavour* by Parkinson entitled 'Wie View of the entrance into the Bay of Aware, Huaheine A.A.' drawn between 17 and 19 July 1769. This sketch shows the naval hoods and, most importantly, the bumpkins. (*British Library*)

Above:
'*Endeavour* at Sea' by Parkinson, depicting the storm of 28 December 1769 off the North Cape of New Zealand. Important points to note in this sketch are the normal-sized mizzen mast and the dead-lights closed over the stern windows, with their hinges shown. (*British Library*)

Endeavour's boats sketched by Parkinson. *Top, left to right*: the longboat with sliding gunter rig; the pinnace with sliding gunter rig; the yawl with sprit rig. *Bottom, left to right*: the longboat with a mixed rig; the longboat with settee rig. (*British Library*)

Endeavour's boats sketched by Parkinson.
Top, left to right: the pinnace with sprit-rigged mast; the longboat, bow and stern views, with a two-masted sprit rig.
Middle: skiff with a single-masted square-sail rig.
Bottom: Maori canoes.
(*British Library*)

THE DRAWINGS

A General arrangement

A1   SHEER PLAN (scale ⅛in = 1ft)

A1

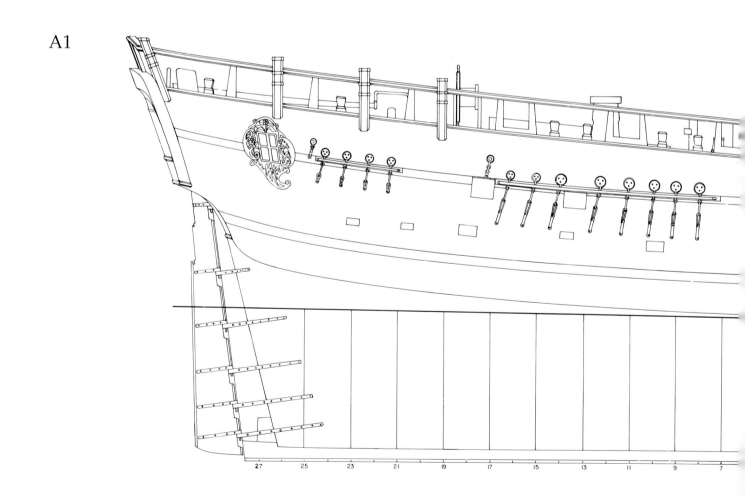

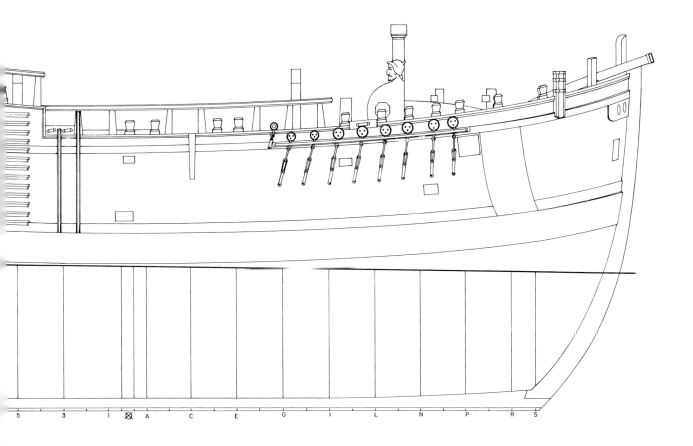

5　　3　　I　⊠　A　　C　　E　　G　　I　　L　　N　　P　R　S

A   General arrangement

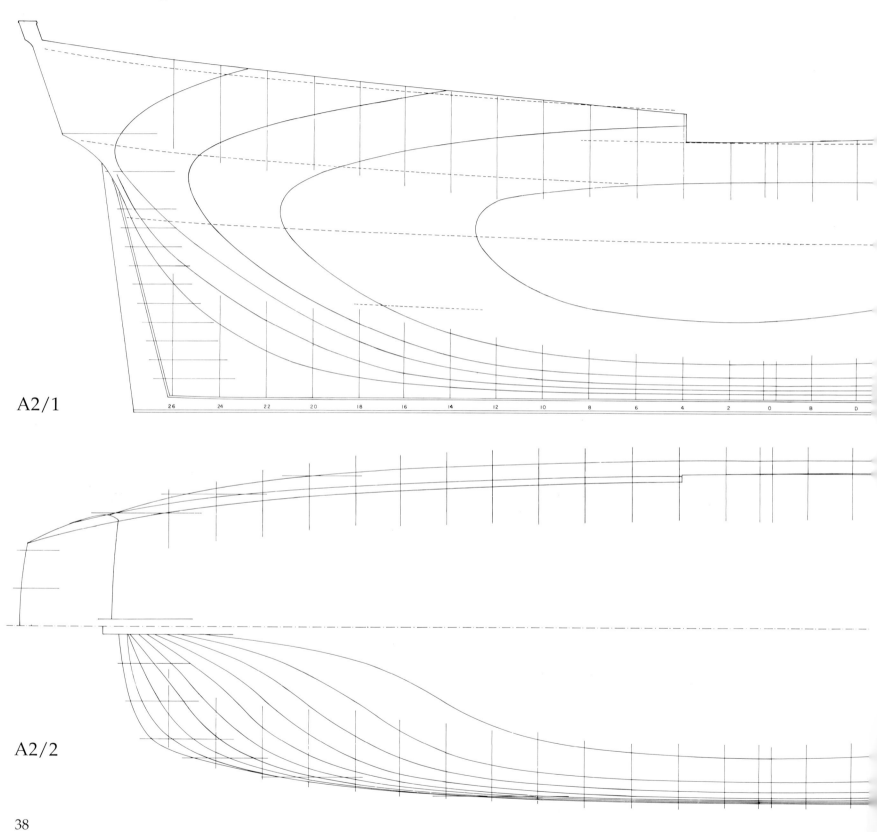

A2/1

A2/2

38

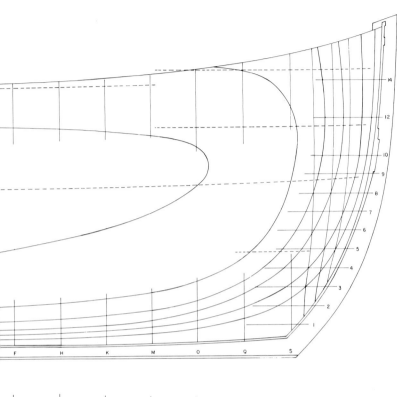

A2   BODY LINES (scale ⅛in = 1ft)

A2/1   Longitudinal

A2/2   Half breadth

A2/3   Cross-sections

A2/3

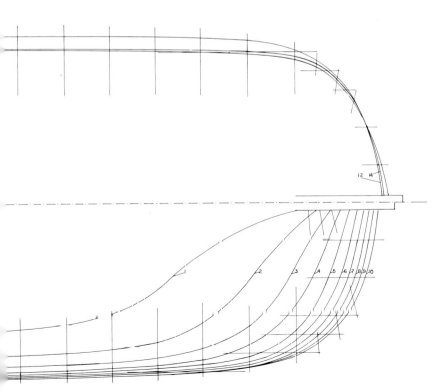

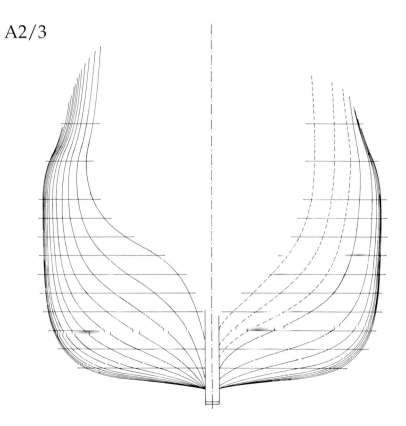

39

A General arrangement

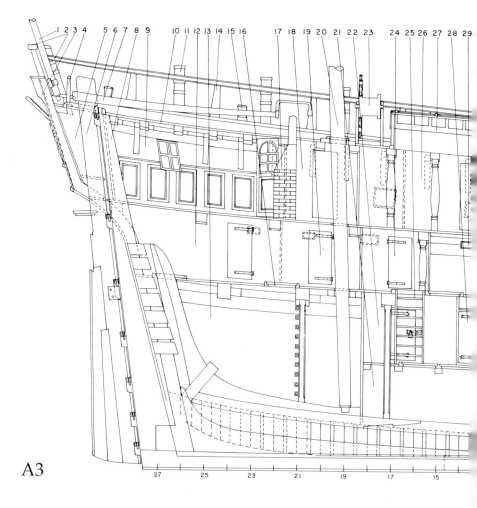

A3

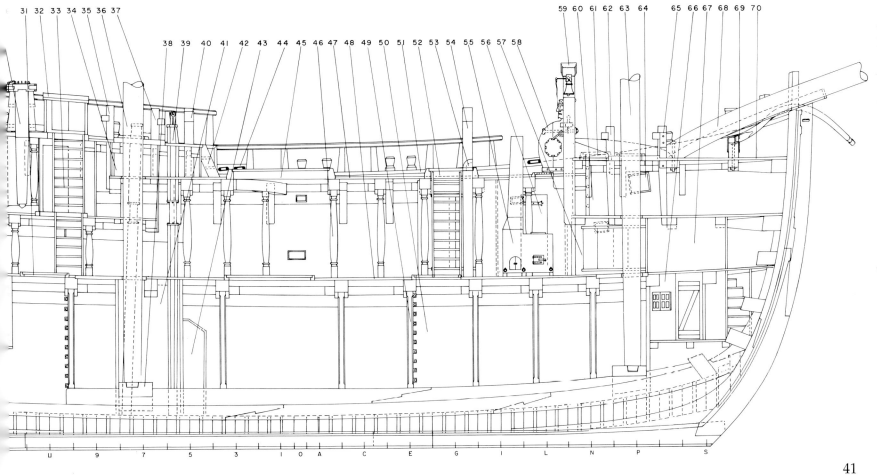

31 32 33 34 35 36 37 59 60 61 62 63 64 65 66 67 68 69 70

38 39 40 41 42 43 44 45 46 47 48 49 50 51 52 53 54 55 56 57 58

U   9   7   5   3   I   O   A   C   E   G   I   L   N   P   S

41

A General arrangement

A4   CROSS-SECTIONS (scale ⅛in = 1ft)

A4/1   Cross-section 0 to E

1   Main hatch-cover
2   Main hatch-coaming
3   Gutter-ledge
4   Binding strakes
5   Upper deck beam
6   Upper deck planks
7   Chine
8   Waterway
9   Spirketting
10   Gunwale
11   Timberhead
12   Toptimber (rail stanchion)
13   Roughtree rail
14   Toptimber
15   Filling plank
16   Sheer strake
17   Airing port

18   Chess-tree
19   Side planks
20   Thickstuff above wales
21   Wales
22   Thickstuff below wales
23   Diminishing strakes
24   Second futtock
25   Bottom planks
26   Floortimber
27   Garboard strake
29   Keel
30   False keel
31   Keelson
32   Deadwood above keelson
33   Deck stanchion
34   Lower deck planks
35   Lower deck binding strakes
36   Lower deck main hatchway
37   Lower deck beam
38   Hold stanchion

39   Upper deck clamp
40   Supporting thickstuff
41   Lower deck ceiling
42   Lower deck waterway
43   Lower deck chine
44   Chocks
45   Lower deck clamp
46   Supporting thickstuff
47   Hold ceiling
48   Thickstuff about the floor-heads
49   Foot-waling
50   Limber strakes
51   Limber board

A4/2   Cross-section E to K

1   Fore hatchway spar gallows
2   Fore hatchway
3   Oven
4   Stairway
5   Hold stanchion steps

6   Fore topgallant backstay iron-bound
      dead eye
7   Fore channel standard
8   Fore shroud dead eye and chain
9   Fore channel
10   Carpenter's cabin

A4/3   Cross-section K to Q

1   Belfry
2   Pawl bit pin
3   Pinrail
4   Fore jeer bits
5   Windlass barrel
6   Spike socket
7   Bit pin
8   Main tack fairlead
9   Standard knee
10   Fore fall
11   Carpenter's store room
12   Oven
13   Foremast step

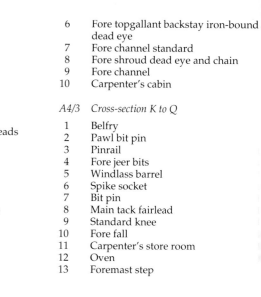

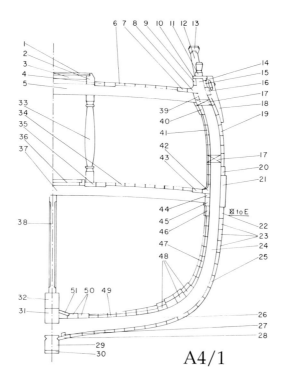

A4/1

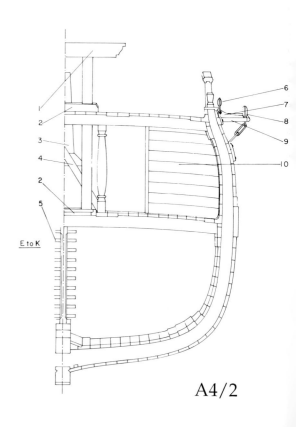

A4/2

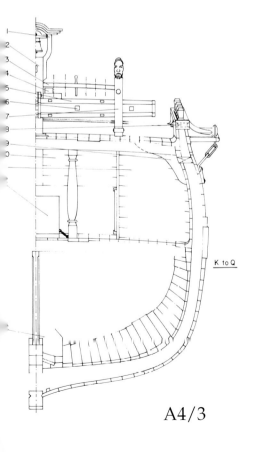

A4/3

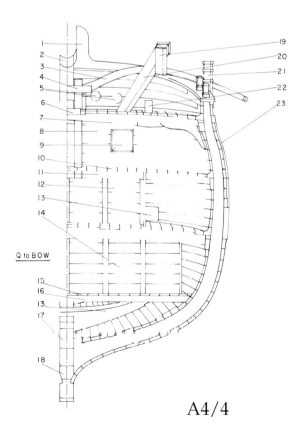

A4/4

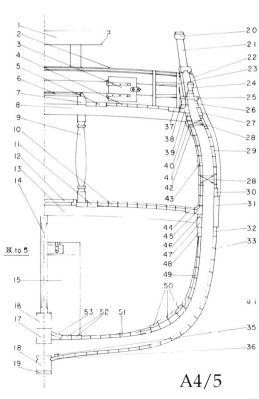

A4/5

A General arrangement

(continued on next page)

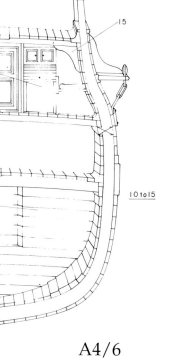

A4/6

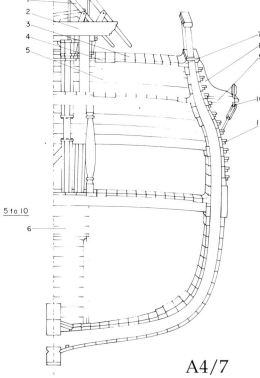

A4/7

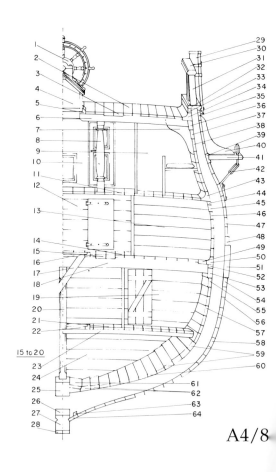

A4/8

52	Chock	6	Surgeon's cabin
53	Lower deck clamp	7	Scuttle to bread room
54	Thickstuff below wales	8	Hold stanchion steps
55	Supporting thickstuff	9	Mizzen channel
56	Diminishing strakes		
57	Hold ceiling		*A4/10 Cross-section 25 to Stern*
58	Bottom planks		
59	Thickstuff about the floor-heads	1	Roughtree rail
60	Foot-waling	2	Stern timber
61	Limber board	3	Bridge rail stanchion
62	Limber strakes	4	Taffarel
63	Limber hole	5	Iron horse
64	Garboard strake	6	Helm (Rudder)
		7	Bridge over the tiller
	A4/9 Cross-section 20 to 25	8	Tiller
		9	Flag lockers
1	Tiller bracket	10	Quarterdeck helmport
2	Cabin flue	11	Great cabin
3	Lobby	12	Lower counter loading port
4	Fire place	13	1st Lieutenant's cabin
5	Captain's bed	14	Messroom
		15	Sternson

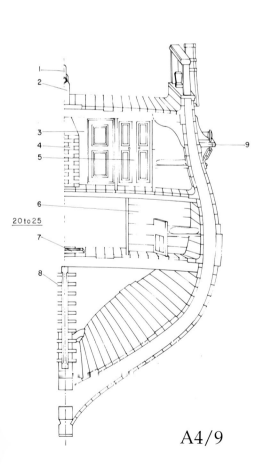

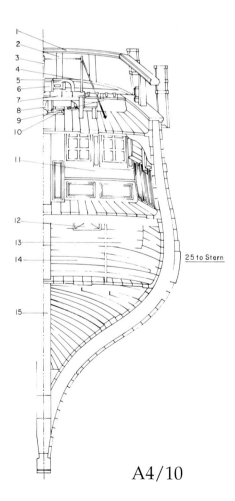

A4/9 A4/10

B Hull structure

B1 FRAME DISPOSITION
(scale ⅛in = 1ft)

1   Stern timber
2   Outer stern timber
3   Timbers on the outer stern timber
4   Fashion piece
5   Window sill
6   Fashion futtock
7   Badge window
8   Overhead filling piece
9   Airing port
10 Light port
11 Port sill
12 Overhead filling piece
13 Gunport
14 Long toptimbers shaped as timber-
    heads
15 Floor timber
16 Second futtock
17 Long top timber shaped as rail
    stanchion
18 Short top timber
19 Third futtock
20 First futtock
21 Filling pieces (knuckle timbers)
22 Hawse pieces
23 Knighthead
24 Wing-transom
25 Transoms
26 Filling chocks

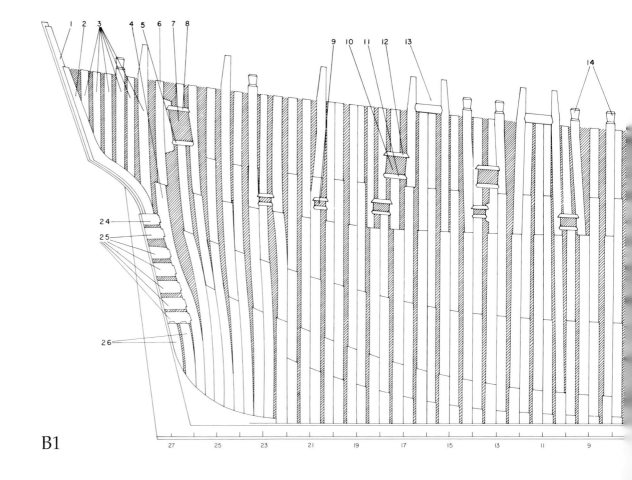

B1

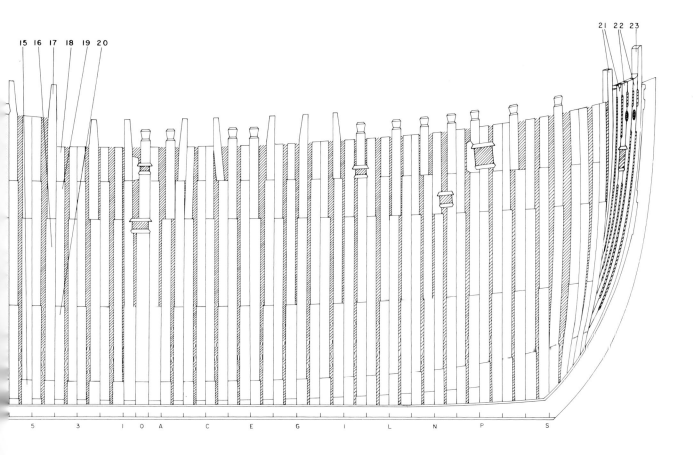

15 16 17 18 19 20

21 22 23

5   3   I   0   A   C   E   G   I   L   N   P   S

B Hull structure

B2

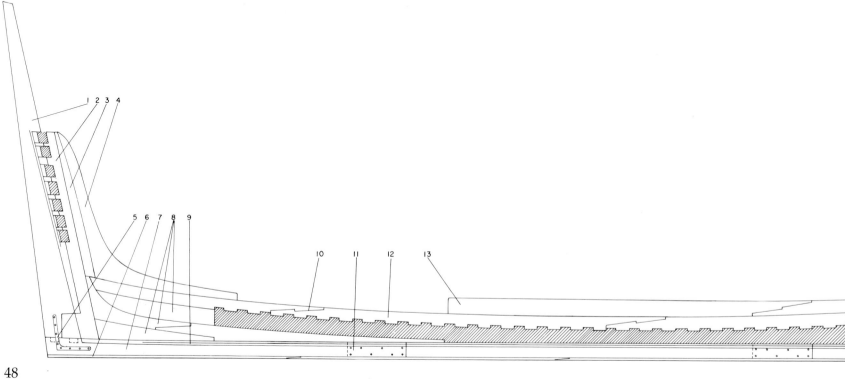

B3

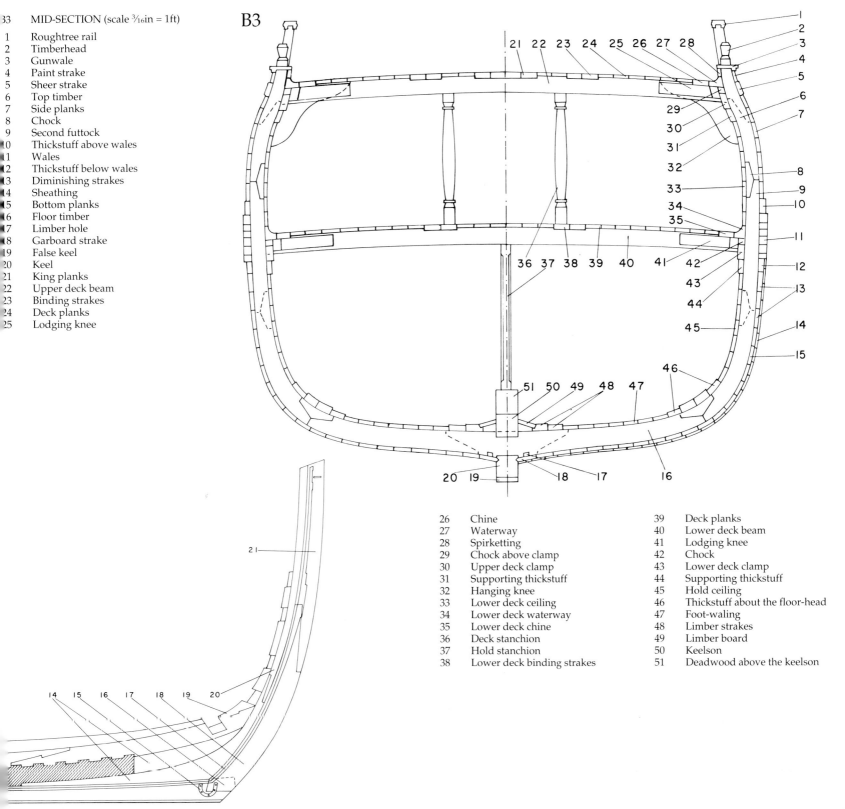

B Hull structure

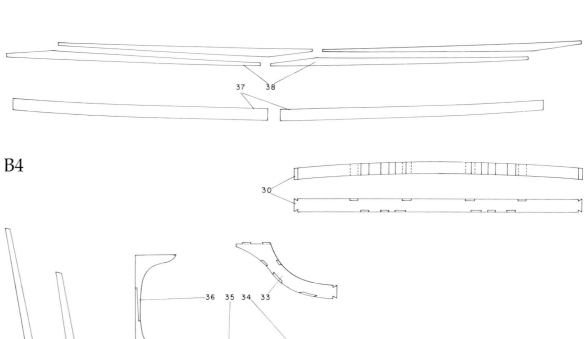

B4

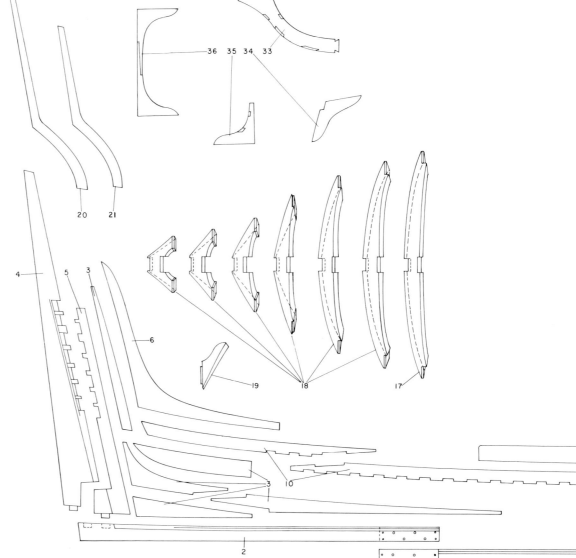

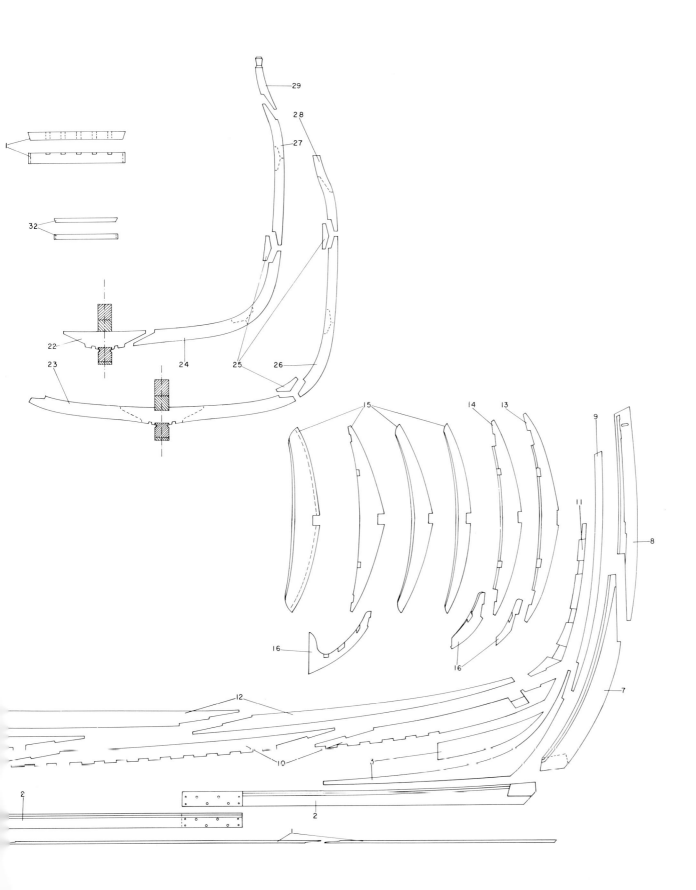

51

B Hull structure

B5 STERN (scale ³/₁₆in = 1ft)

B5/1 Construction

1 Roughtree rail
2 Gun stock
3 Stern timber or long counter timber
4 Taffarel
5 Chock
6 Beam above windows
7 Outer stern timber

8 Window sill beam
9 Short counter timbers
10 Counter-beam
11 Helmport chocks
12 Filling piece
13 Filling piece
14 Wing-transom
15 Fashion piece
16 Transoms
17 Filling chocks

B5/2 Stern timbers with dead-light and port

1 Cleat
2 Roughtree rail
3 Stern timber
4 Taffarel capping
5 Taffarel
6 Quarterdeck end beam
7 Dead-light
8 Window

9 Short counter timber
10 Stern port lid
11 Stern loading or light port
12 Wing-transom
13 Transoms
14 Filling chocks
15 Sternpost
16 Inner sternpost
17 Deadwood
18 Keel

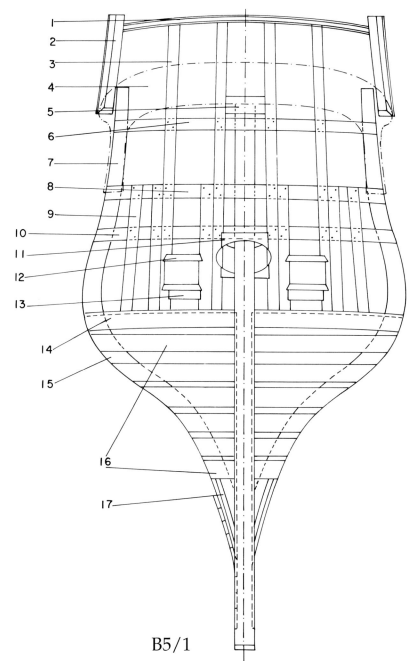

B5/1

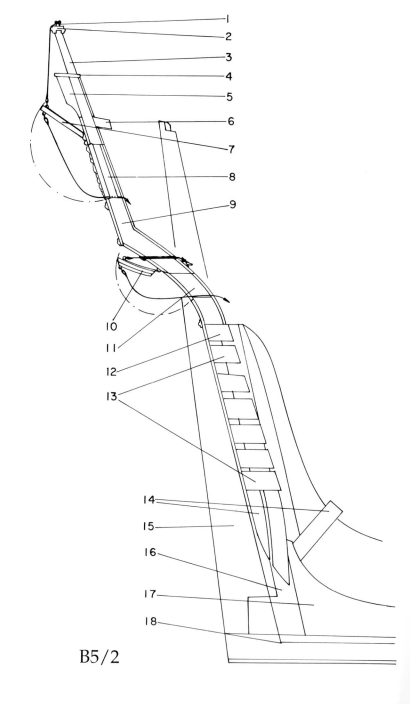

B5/2

B6　BOW TIMBERS (scale 3/16in = 1ft)

1　Short top timber
2　Long top timber
3　Third futtock
4　Second futtock
5　Futtock of the crotch
6　Crotch
7　Filling pieces
8　Hawse pieces
9　Knighthead or bollard timber
10　Stem

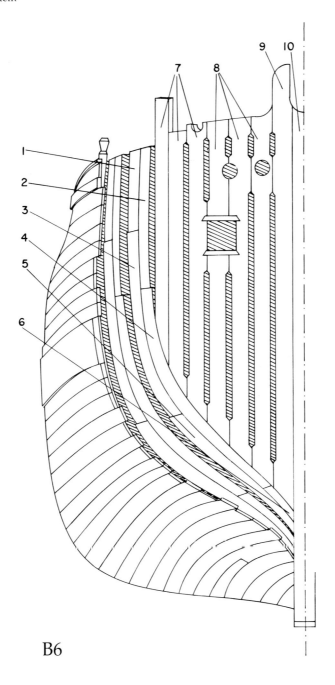

B6

C External hull

C1

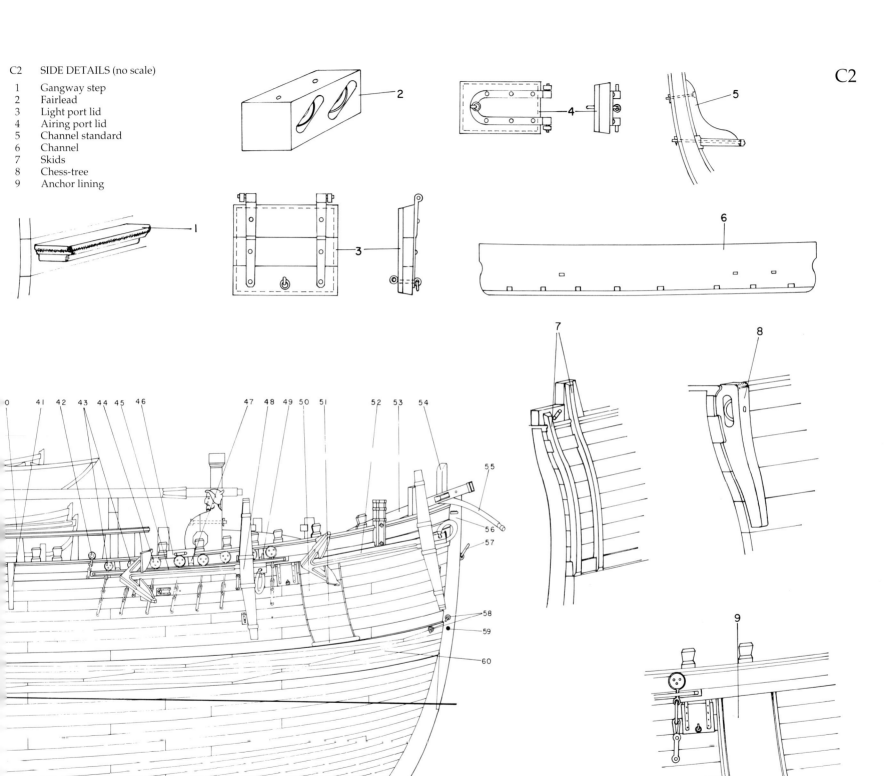

C2   SIDE DETAILS (no scale)

1   Gangway step
2   Fairlead
3   Light port lid
4   Airing port lid
5   Channel standard
6   Channel
7   Skids
8   Chess-tree
9   Anchor lining

C2

55

C External hull

C3   UPPER DECK PLAN
      (scale ⅛in = 1ft)

1   Swivel gun
2   Cleat for dead-light rope
3   Roughtree rail above taffarel
4   Taffarel
5   Lantern
6   Ensign staff bracket
7   Stern timber
8   Flag locker
9   Ensign staff step
10   Iron horse
11   Helmport
12   Helm (rudder)
13   Bridge over tiller
14   Tiller
15   King planks
16   Deck planks

17   Binding strake
18   Mizzen channel
19   Quarterdeck roughtree rail
20   Swivel gun stock
21   Mizzen channel standard
22   Quarterdeck waterway
23   Fireplace flue
24   Mizzen mast partners
25   Steering wheel
26   Binnacle
27   Skylight
28   Bracket for main studding sail boom
29   Main channel standard
30   Main channel
31   Quarterdeck
32   Capstan
33   Companion capping
34   Main jeer bits

35   Mainmast partners
36   Lower main studding sail boom
37   Gooseneck bracket
38   Pump
39   Main topsail sheet bits
40   Gangway
41   Quarterdeck spar gallows
42   Quarterdeck steps
43   Sheets fairlead
44   Skids
45   Main hatchway
46   4-pounder carriage gun
47   Waist roughtree rail
48   Chine
49   Chess-tree
50   Fore hatch hood
51   Fore hatch spar gallows
52   Fore channel

53   Fore channel standard
54   Oven flue
55   Tack fairlead
56   Windlass
57   Timberhead
58   Scuttle to fore fall
59   Fore jeer bits
60   Foremast partners
61   Davit shackle
62   Probable lower fore studding sail
      boom position
63   Fore topsail sheet bits
64   Bumpkin bracket
65   Forecastle
66   Bumpkin
67   Cat-head
68   Knighthead
69   Stem
70   Gammoning ring

C3

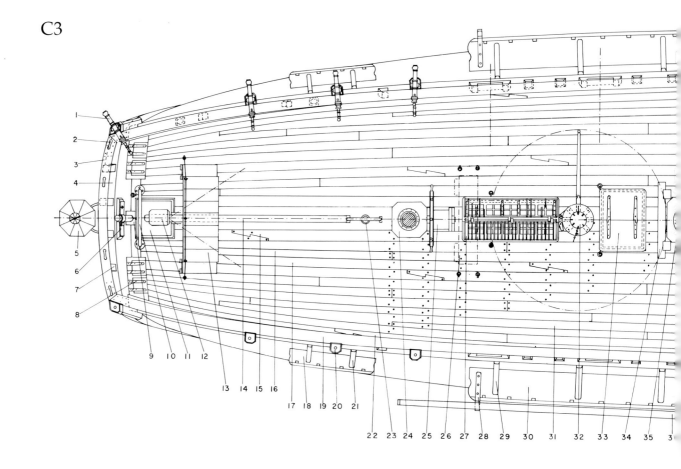

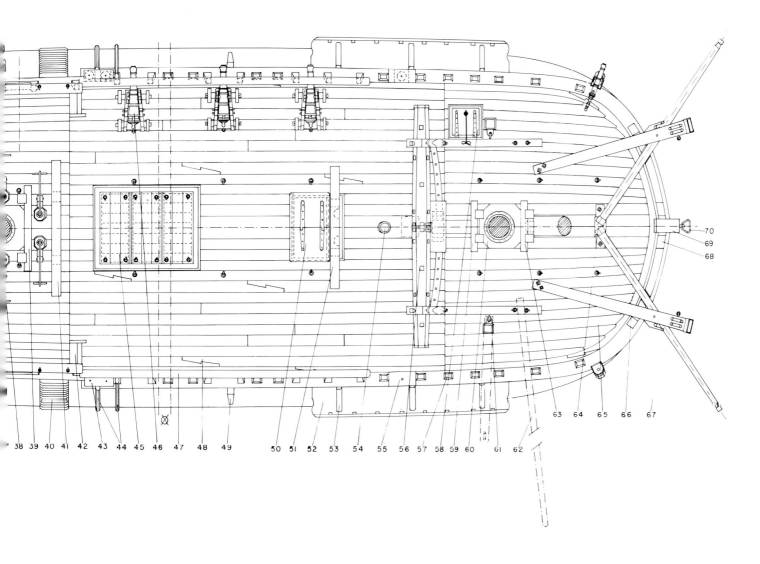

38 39 40 41 42 43 44 45 46 47 48 49 50 51 52 53 54 55 56 57 58 59 60 61 62 63 64 65 66 67

68
69
70

C External hull

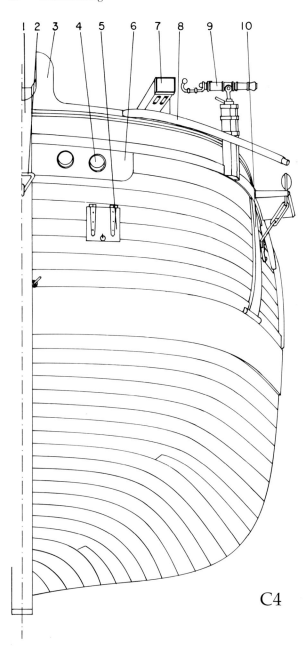

C4

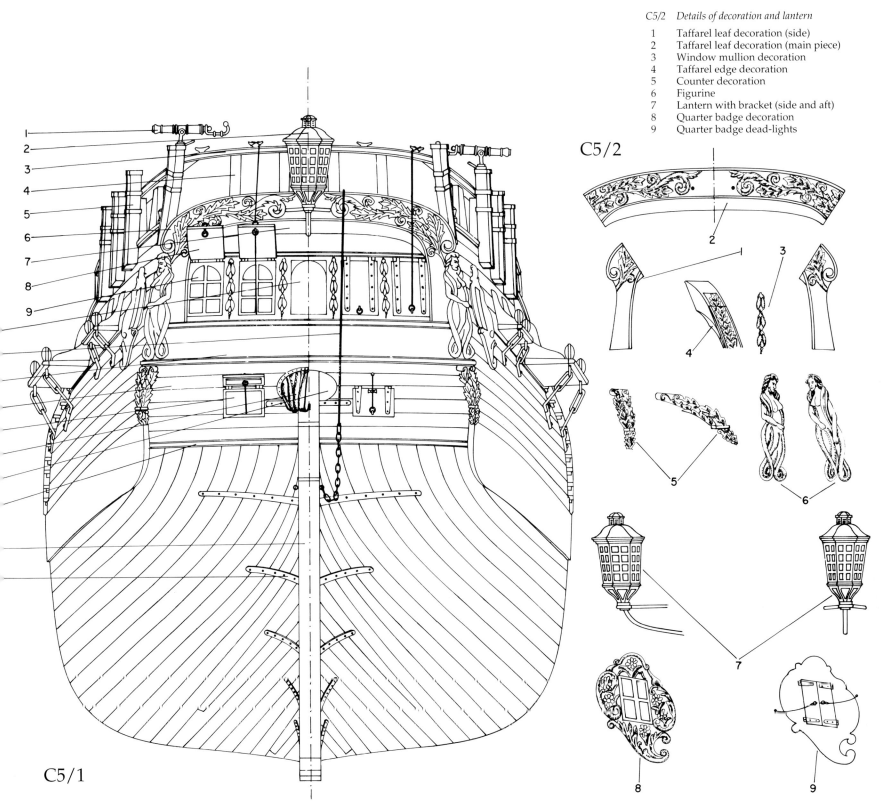

1   Taffarel leaf decoration (side)
2   Taffarel leaf decoration (main piece)
3   Window mullion decoration
4   Taffarel edge decoration
5   Counter decoration
6   Figurine
7   Lantern with bracket (side and aft)
8   Quarter badge decoration
9   Quarter badge dead-lights

C5/2

C5/1

D Internal hull

D1 UPPER DECK, QUARTERDECK
    AND FORECASTLE BEAM
    STRUCTURE (scale ⅛in = 1ft)

1   Quarterdeck end beam
2   Lodging knee
3   Clamp and chock
4   Quarterdeck beam
5   Carlings
6   Half beams or ledges
7   Hanging knee
8   Upper deck beam
9   Spur beam
10 Forecastle deck beam
11 Forecastle deck hook

D1

D2 FORE FALL (scale ⅛in = 1ft)

1   Light port
2   Bow loading port
3   Fore topsail sheet bits
4   Decks hook
5   Carling
6   Half beam or ledge
7   Fore fall deck beam
8   Hook extension
9   Lodging knee
10 Fore jeer bits
11 Pawl bit

D2

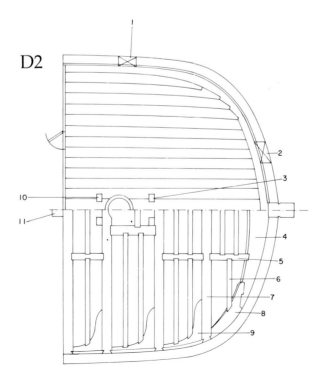

60

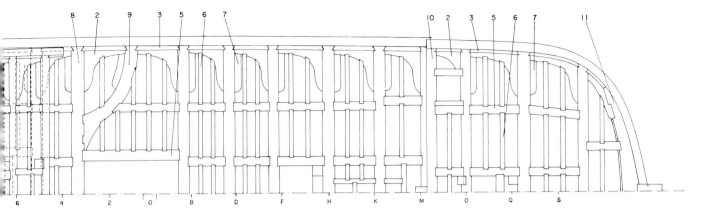

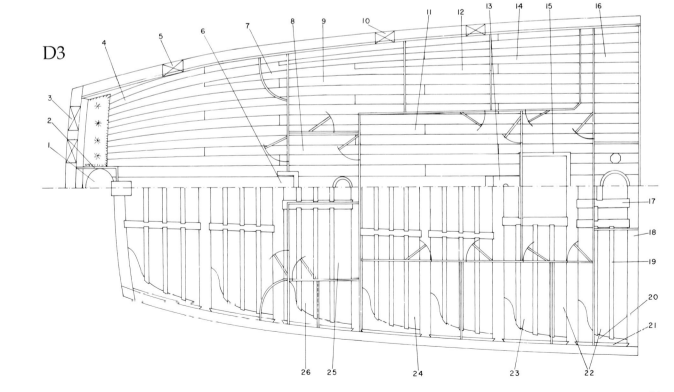

D Internal hull

D4 LOWER DECK

D4/1 *Plan (scale ⅛in = 1ft)*

1 Stern loading port
2 Mess room
3 Scuttle to bread room
4 1st Lieutenant's cabin
5 Surgeon's cabin
6 Airing port
7 Gunner's cabin
8 Ladderway to steward's room
9 After hatchway
10 Pump
11 Main hatchway
12 Fore hatchway
13 Sail room
14 Oven
15 Boatswain's cabin
16 Boatswain's store room
17 Sail room
18 Passage to magazine
19 Gunner's store
20 Breast hook
21 Carling
22 Half-beam or ledge
23 Lower deck beam
24 Lodging knee
25 Lower deck clamp
26 Carpenter's store room
27 Carpenter's cabin
28 Midship lodging knees
29 Cabin of the Captain's clerk
30 2nd Lieutenant's cabin
31 Master's cabin
32 Transom
33 Scuttle

D4/1

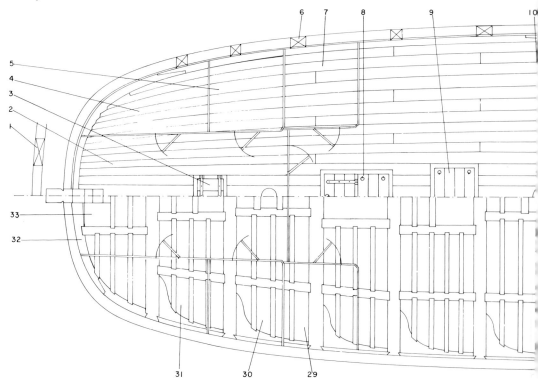

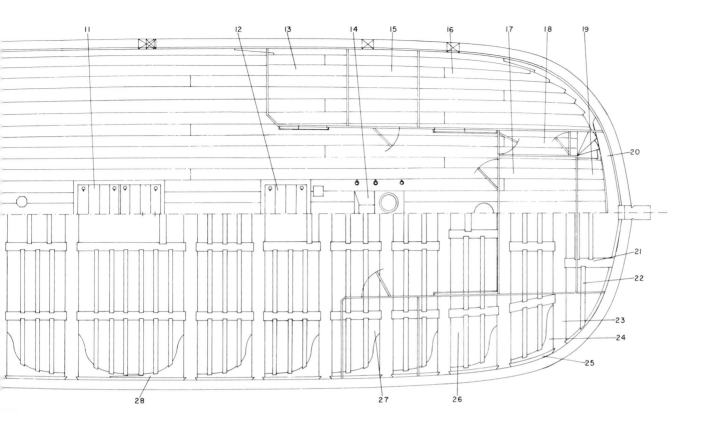

D4/2 *View aft towards the officers' quarters below the cabin deck (no scale)*

D4/2

D4/3 *View forward showing oven, fore fall, sail room and passage to magazine (no scale)*

D4/3

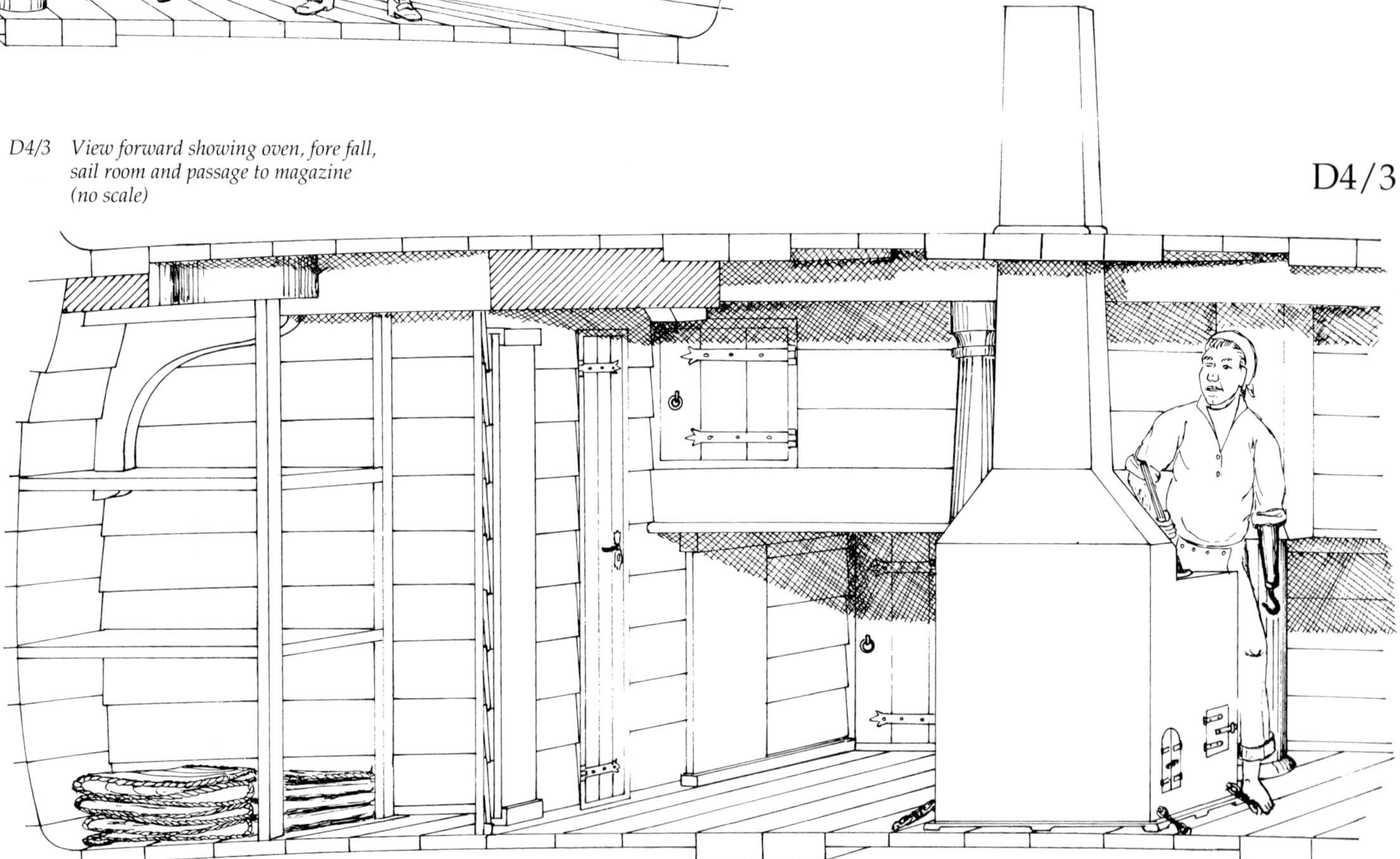

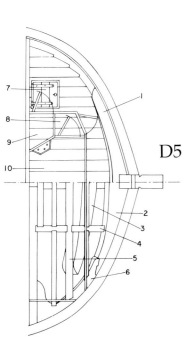

D5

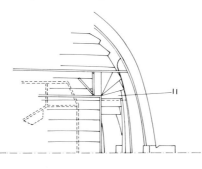

D5   MAGAZINE PLATFORM
(scale ⅛in = 1ft)

1   3rd breast hook
2   2nd breast hook
3   Lowest breast hook
4   Carling
5   Platform beam
6   3rd hook's extension
7   Scuttle
8   Magazine entrance
9   Light room
10   Magazine
11   Magazine stairway

D6   PUMP WELL AND STEWARD'S
ROOM PLATFORM
(scale ⅛in = 1ft)

1   Pump
2   Main mast step
3   Keelson
4   Well
5   Shot locker
6   Slops room
7   Steward's room
8   Scuttle and hatchway to fishroom
9   Carling
10   Half-beam or ledge
11   Platform beam
12   Lodging knee

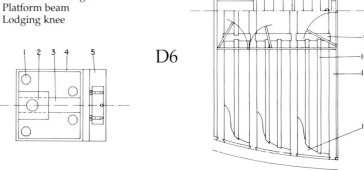

D6

D7   THE USE OF SPIKES ETC. ON LIVE
AND DEAD WORK
(scale ⅛in = 1ft)

1   Bolt
2   Trennel
3   Spike

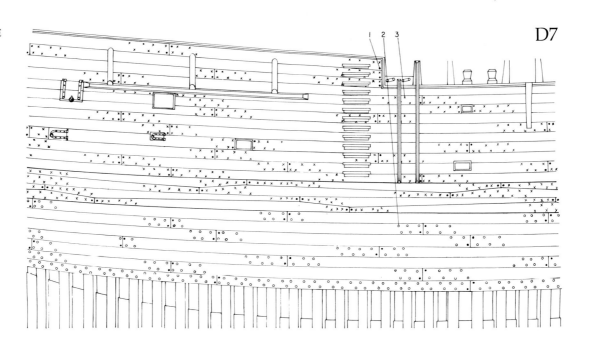

D7

E Fittings

E1   INSIDE TAFFAREL
(scale ³⁄₁₆in = 1ft)

1   Taffarel
2   Flag locker
3   Iron horse
4   Ensign staff bracket
5   Ensign staff step
6   Helmport
7   Quarterdeck

E1

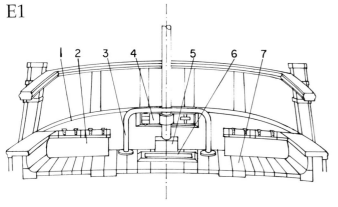

E2   PLATFORM OVER TILLER AND
UPPER HELMPORT COAT
(no scale)

1   Platform over the tiller
2   Stanchion and hand rope
3   Helm with a rudder coat closing the
quarterdeck helmport

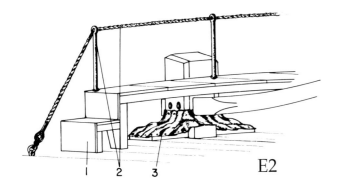

E2

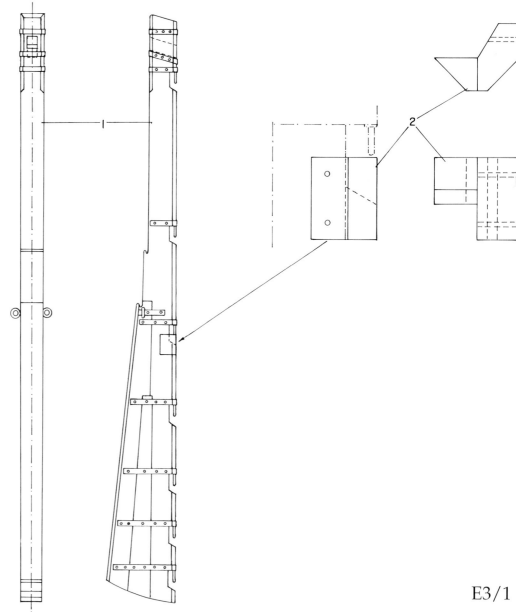

E3/1

E3   STEERING GEAR

E3/1   Rudder (scale ³⁄₁₆in = 1ft)

1   Rudder with pintles etc.
2   Woodlock (4 x enlarged)
3   Pintle and gudgeon (rudder brace)
     with copper washer (3 x enlarged)
4   Rudder coat
5   Rudder pendant

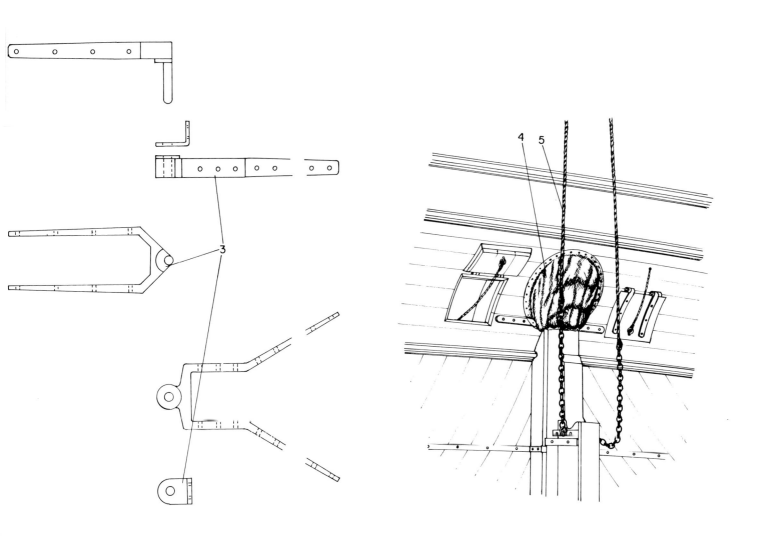

E   Fittings

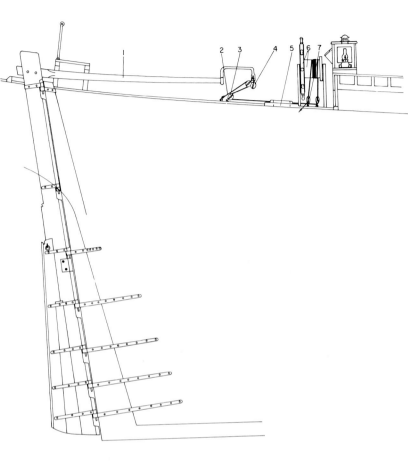

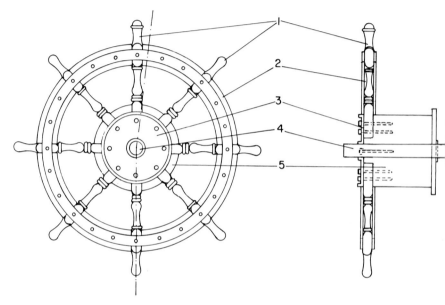

E3/2   *Steering arrangement (elevation and plan) (scale ⅛in = 1ft)*

1   Tiller
2   Tiller rope
3   Waterway foot block
4   Tiller blocks
5   Mizzenmast partners
6   Steering wheel
7   Barrel foot block

E3/3   *Steering wheel (no scale)*

1   Spokes
2   Felloes
3   Hub
4   Axle
5   Barrel
6   Support post
7   Barrel with five turns of tiller rope and foot blocks. The middle rope nailed on top to the barrel

E3/2

E3/3

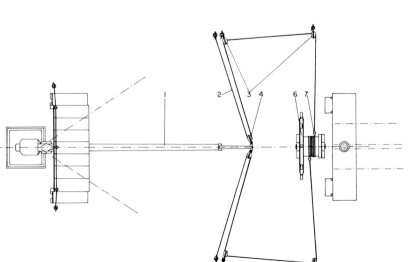

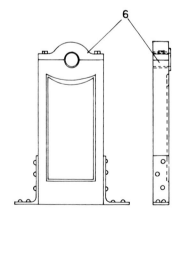

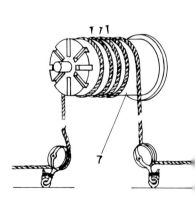

E3/4   *Navigational implements (no scale)*

1   Binnacle
2   Compass compartment
3   Drawer for charts etc.
4   Lamp compartment
5   Skylight
6   Lashings of the binnacle to the deck
7   Compass
8   Half hour glass
9   Binnacle lamp

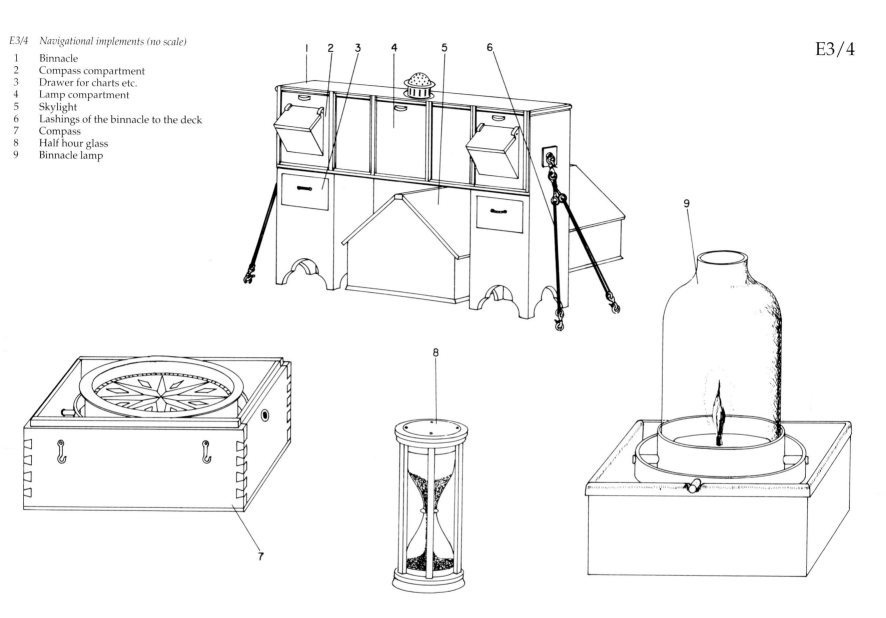

E   Fittings

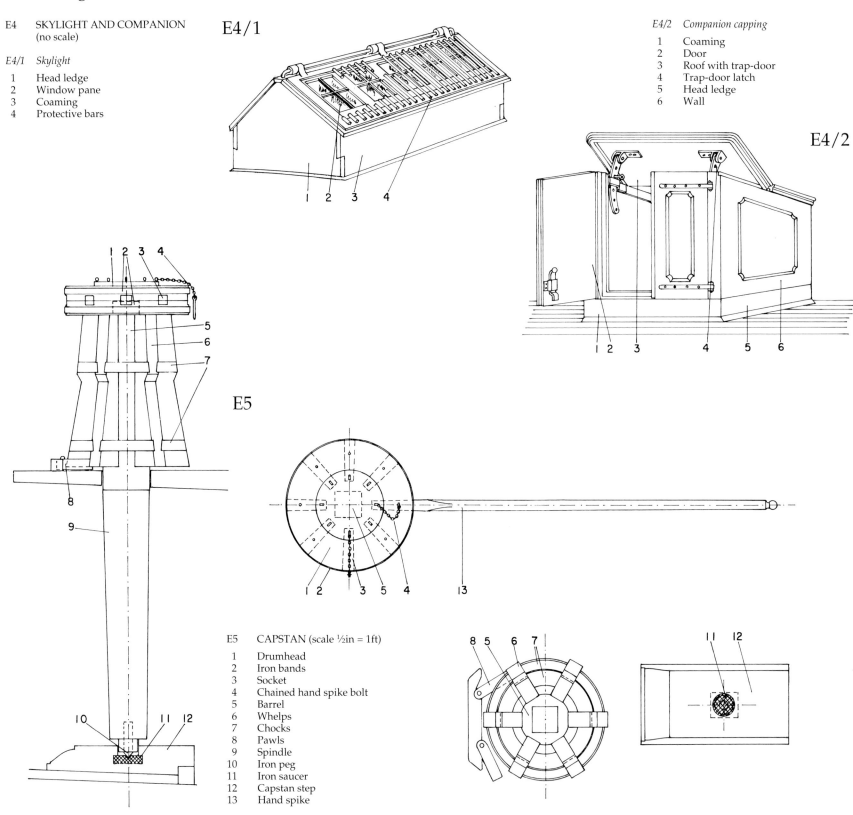

E4   SKYLIGHT AND COMPANION
(no scale)

E4/1   Skylight

1   Head ledge
2   Window pane
3   Coaming
4   Protective bars

E4/1

E4/2   Companion capping

1   Coaming
2   Door
3   Roof with trap-door
4   Trap-door latch
5   Head ledge
6   Wall

E4/2

E5

E5   CAPSTAN (scale ½in = 1ft)

1   Drumhead
2   Iron bands
3   Socket
4   Chained hand spike bolt
5   Barrel
6   Whelps
7   Chocks
8   Pawls
9   Spindle
10   Iron peg
11   Iron saucer
12   Capstan step
13   Hand spike

E6   PUMPS (scale ⅜in = 1ft)

1   Brake
2   Spear
3   Forked stanchion
4   Iron bands
5   Canvas hose
6   Canvas coating over deck opening
7   Raising pipe
8   Pump chamber
9   Woolding
10   Suction pipe
11   Basket
12   Pump shoe
13   Pump bucket

E7   MAINMAST BITS (no scale)

1   Main topsail sheet bits
2   Bit pin
3   Cross-piece
4   Sheaves
5   Main jeer bits
6   Quarterdeck beam
7   Upper deck beam

E6

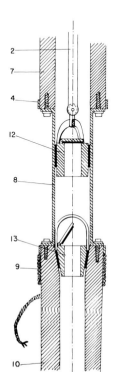

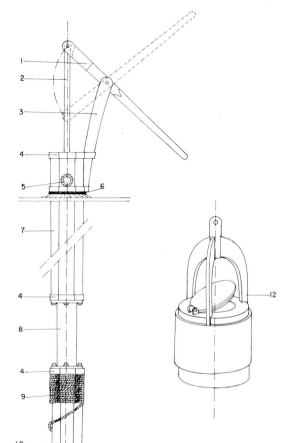

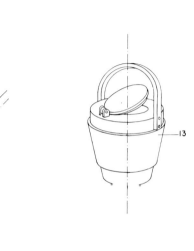

E7

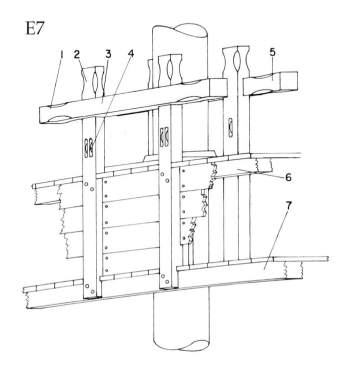

E Fittings

E8 SPAR AND BOAT GALLOWS ON
QUARTERDECK (no scale)

1 Gallows
2 Quarterdeck beam
3 Forward bulkhead
4 Upper deck beam
5 Manhole

E8

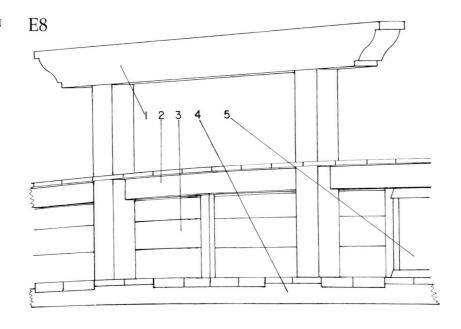

E9 HATCHES (no scale)

E9/1 *Main hatchway*

1 Hatch or hatch cover
2 Hatch coaming
3 Gutter-ledge
4 Hatch head ledge
5 Tarpaulin
6 Hatch bar with lock
7 Hatch battens

E9/1

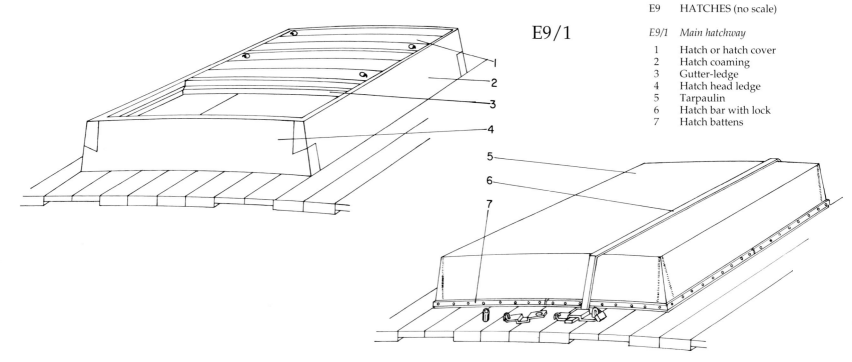

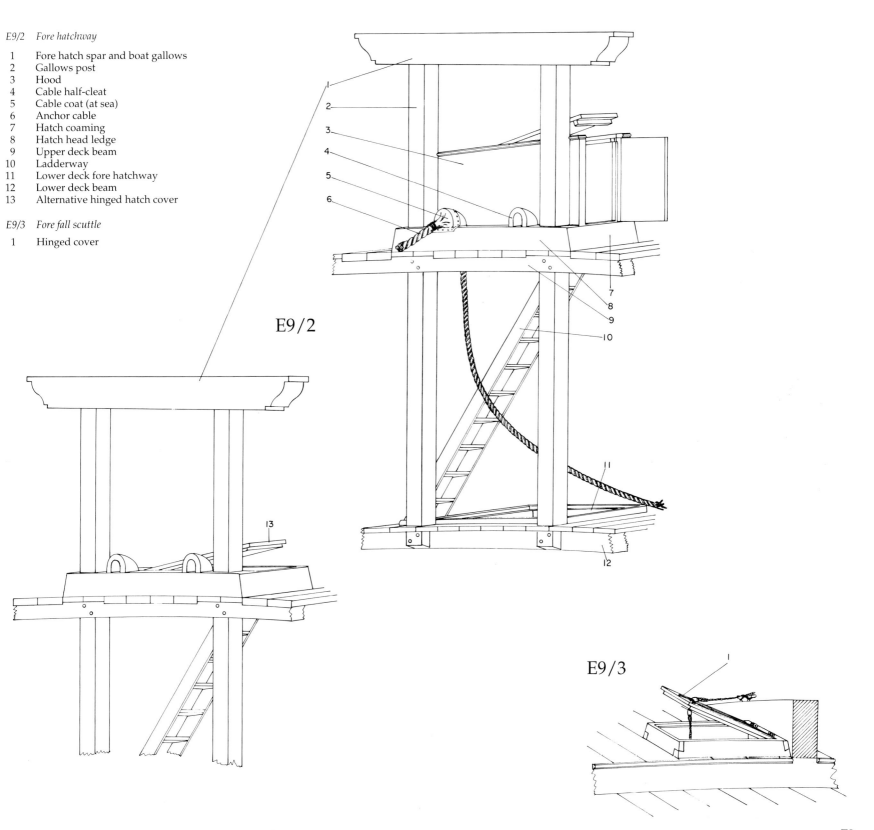

E9/2 *Fore hatchway*

1 Fore hatch spar and boat gallows
2 Gallows post
3 Hood
4 Cable half-cleat
5 Cable coat (at sea)
6 Anchor cable
7 Hatch coaming
8 Hatch head ledge
9 Upper deck beam
10 Ladderway
11 Lower deck fore hatchway
12 Lower deck beam
13 Alternative hinged hatch cover

E9/3 *Fore fall scuttle*

1 Hinged cover

E9/2

E9/3

E Fittings

E10

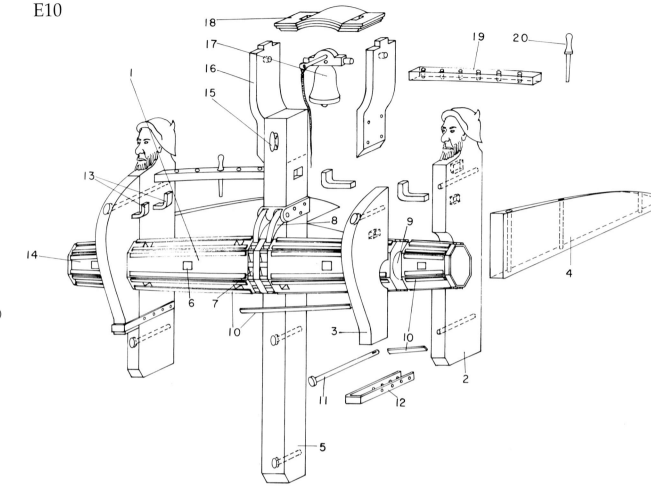

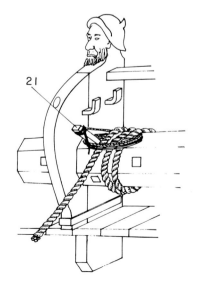

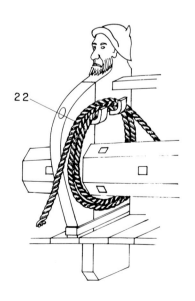

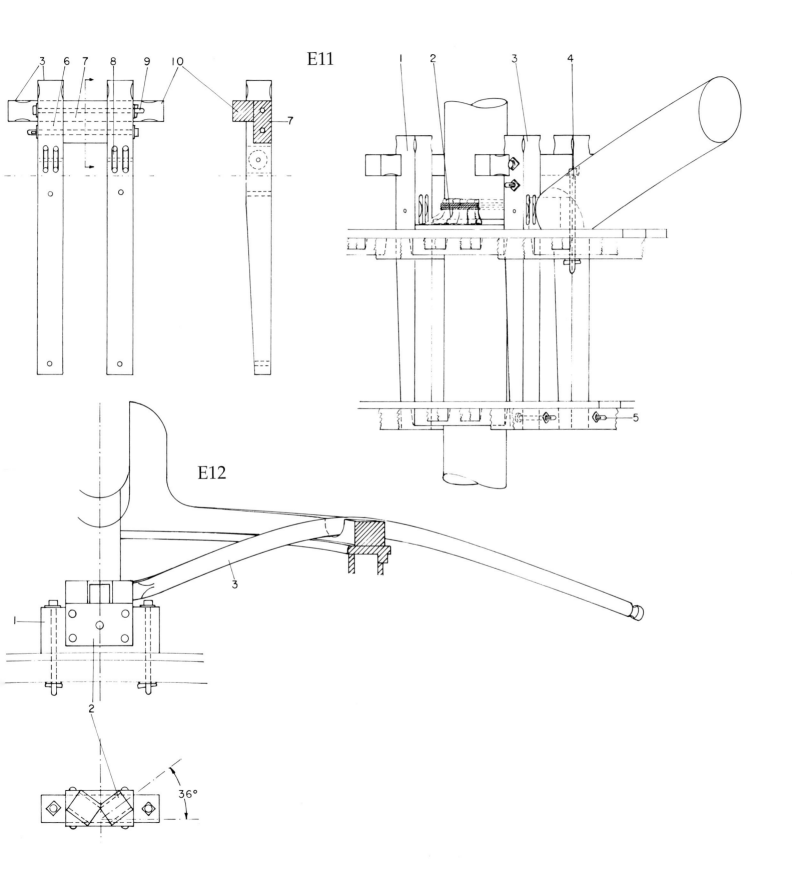

E11

E12

E Fittings

E13 ANCHORS AND ANCHOR
      TACKLE

E13/1 *Anchors (scale ³⁄₁₆in = 1ft)*

1   Sheet anchor and bower
2   Anchor ring
3   Anchor stock
4   Hoops
5   Nuts
6   Anchor shank or shaft
7   Anchor flukes
8   Anchor arm
9   Anchor crown
10   Stream anchor (stock not shown)
11   Kedge anchor (stock not shown)

E13/1

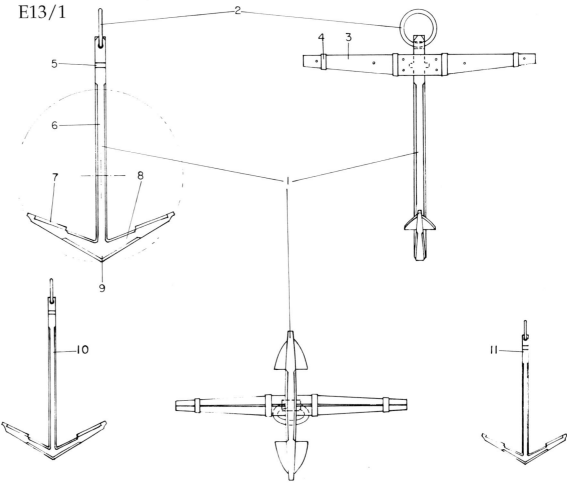

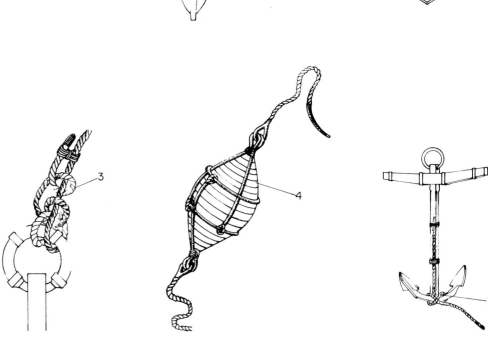

E13/2 *Puddening, knots etc. (no scale)*

1   Puddening of a ring
2   Cable clinch for larger anchors
3   Fisherman's bend for kedge anchors
4   Anchor buoy with a buoy-rope at
     the lower end and a short buoy
     lanyard at the upper
5   Buoy-rope connected to an anchor's
     shaft and crown

E13/2

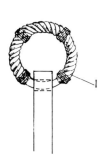

E13/3

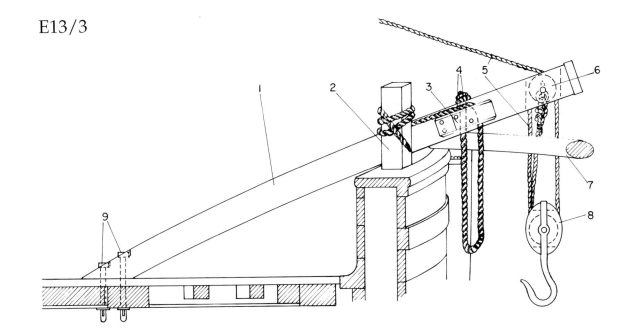

E13/4

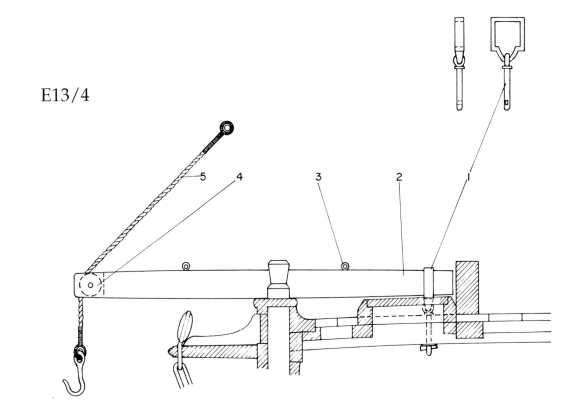

E Fittings

E13/5 Anchors stowed (scale ⅛in = 1ft)

1   Small bower
2   Shank-painter
3   Sheet anchor
4   Cat-head stopper

E13/6 Anchor cable from lower deck to hawse
hole (scale ⅛in = 1ft)

1   Cable
2   Half-cleat
3   Windlass barrel
4   Hawse hole

E13/5

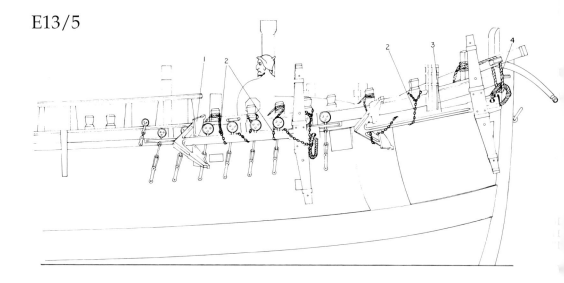

E13/6

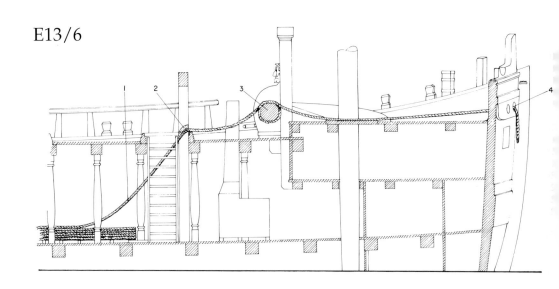

F Armament

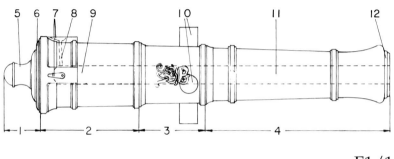

F1/1

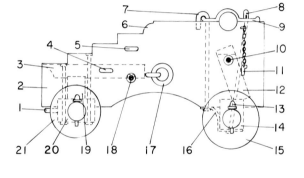

F1/2

F1 CARRIAGE GUNS (scale ¾in = 1ft)

F1/1 *4-pounder gun, side elevation and plan*

1 Cascable
2 First reinforcement
3 Second reinforcement
4 Chase
5 Butt
6 Breech
7 Pan
8 Vent
9 Chamber
10 Trunnion
11 Bore
12 Muzzle

F1/2 *Gun carriage, side elevation and plan*

1 Train tackle eyebolt
2 Bracket
3 Stool bed
4 Gun tackle eyebolt
5 Gun tackle eyebolt
6 Quadrant
7 Capsquare eyebolt
8 Capsquare joint-bolt
9 Capsquare
10 Transom bolt
11 Capsquare key
12 Transom
13 Linch pin
14 Fore axtree
15 Fore truck
16 Axtree stay
17 Breeching ring-bolt
18 Bed-bolt
19 Bolster
20 Rear or hind axtree
21 Rear or hind truck
22 Axtree hoop
23 Bracket bolts

F1/3 *Mounted 4-pounder gun*

1 Train tackle
2 Breeching
3 Gun tackle
4 Tompion
5 Quoin
6 Quoin underlay

F1/3

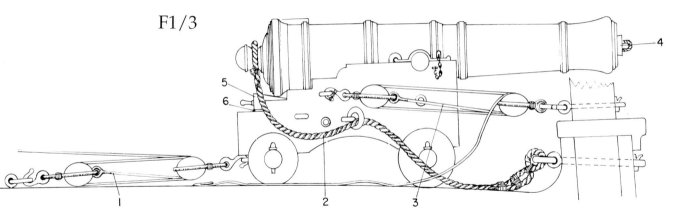

F Armament

F1/4   Ammunition and gun equipment

1   Cartridge bag
2   Round shot
3   Wad
4   Tompion
5   Quoin
6   Quoin underlay
7   Rammer
8   Sponge
9   Ladle
10 Worm
11 Crowbar
12 Gun emblem GEORGE III

F1/4

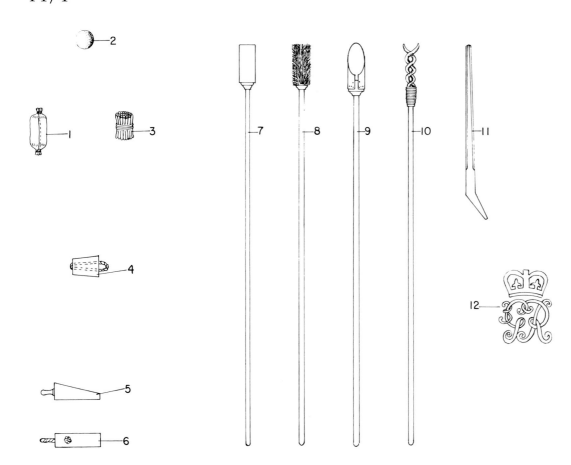

F2   SWIVEL GUNS (scale ¾in = 1ft)

F2/1   *Swivel gun*

1   Swivel gun with upward bent
     handle
2   Swivel gun with fork and
     downward pointing handle
3   Gun fork with semicircular rest for
     loading and securing

F2/1

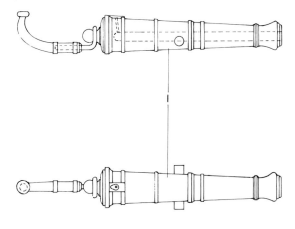

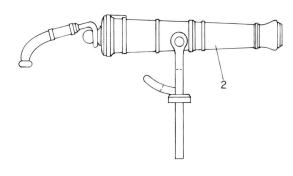

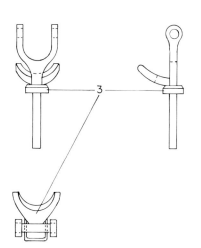

F2/2   *Mounted swivel gun*

1   Swivel gun
2   Handle
3   Fork
4   Iron plate inserted in stock
5   Gun stock

F2/2

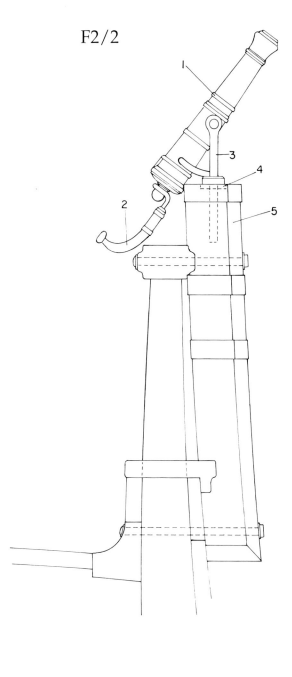

G1   FULLY-RIGGED SHIP
         (scale $\frac{1}{16}$in = 1ft)

G1

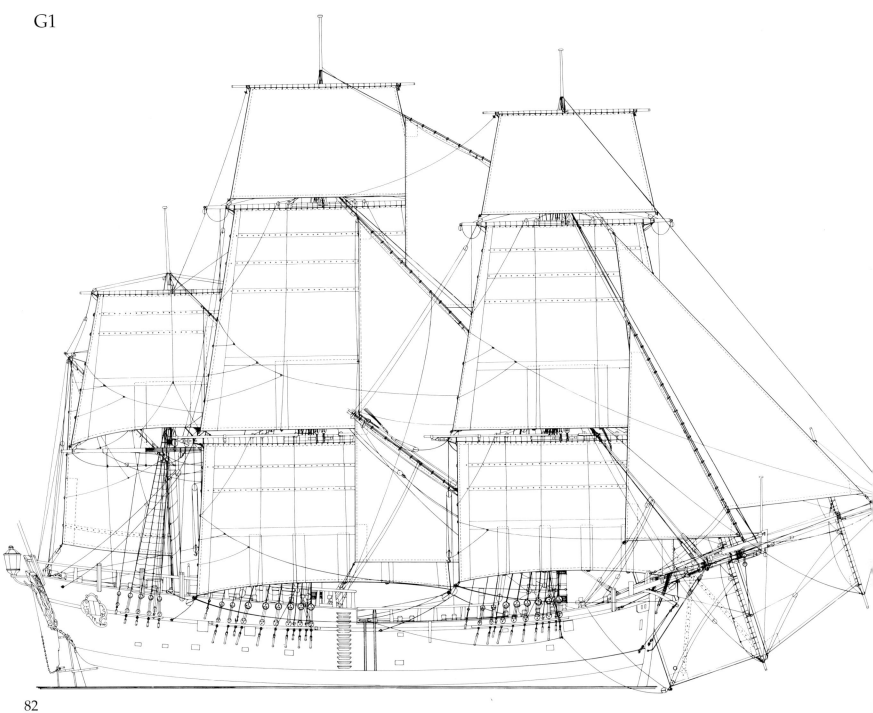

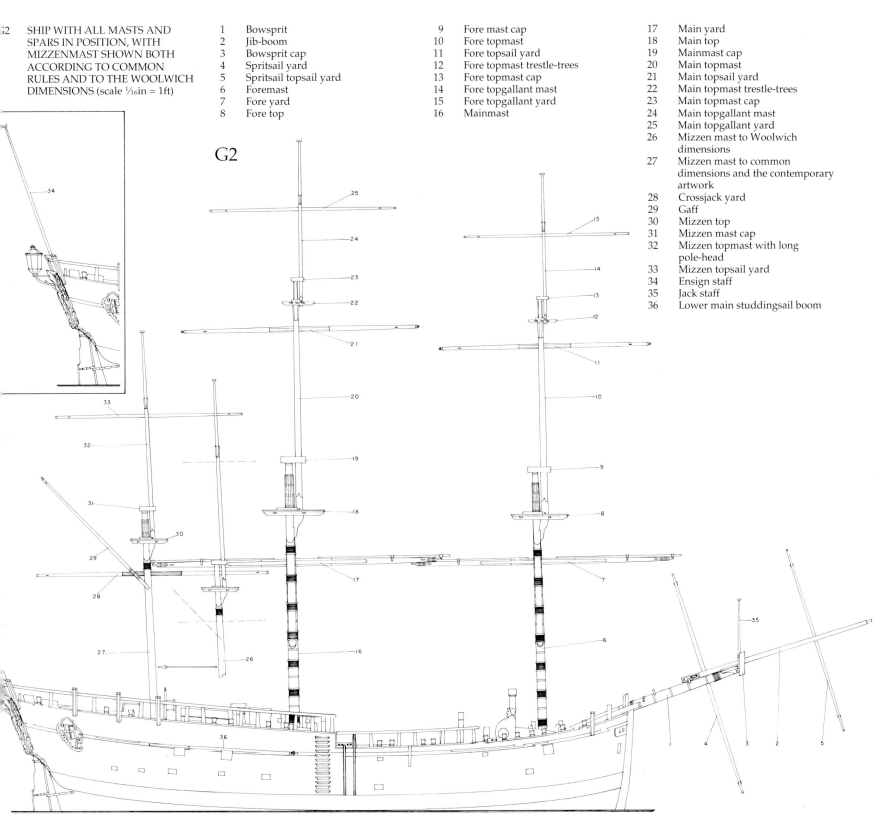

G2   SHIP WITH ALL MASTS AND
      SPARS IN POSITION, WITH
      MIZZENMAST SHOWN BOTH
      ACCORDING TO COMMON
      RULES AND TO THE WOOLWICH
      DIMENSIONS (scale $\frac{1}{16}$in = 1ft)

1	Bowsprit
2	Jib-boom
3	Bowsprit cap
4	Spritsail yard
5	Spritsail topsail yard
6	Foremast
7	Fore yard
8	Fore top
9	Fore mast cap
10	Fore topmast
11	Fore topsail yard
12	Fore topmast trestle-trees
13	Fore topmast cap
14	Fore topgallant mast
15	Fore topgallant yard
16	Mainmast
17	Main yard
18	Main top
19	Mainmast cap
20	Main topmast
21	Main topsail yard
22	Main topmast trestle-trees
23	Main topmast cap
24	Main topgallant mast
25	Main topgallant yard
26	Mizzen mast to Woolwich dimensions
27	Mizzen mast to common dimensions and the contemporary artwork
28	Crossjack yard
29	Gaff
30	Mizzen top
31	Mizzen mast cap
32	Mizzen topmast with long pole-head
33	Mizzen topsail yard
34	Ensign staff
35	Jack staff
36	Lower main studdingsail boom

G2

G Masts and yards

G3 LOWER MASTS

G3/1

G3/1 *Mainmast (side and rear) and foremast (front and side) (scale ⅛in = 1ft)*

1   Cap tenon
2   Masthead
3   Masthead hoop
4   Bib
5   Woolding (13 turns)
6   Woolding timber hoop
7   Mast hoop
8   Cheek
9   Mainmast (side and rear)
10   Mast heel
11   Cheek hoop
12   Hounds
13   Foremast (front)
14   Foremast (side)

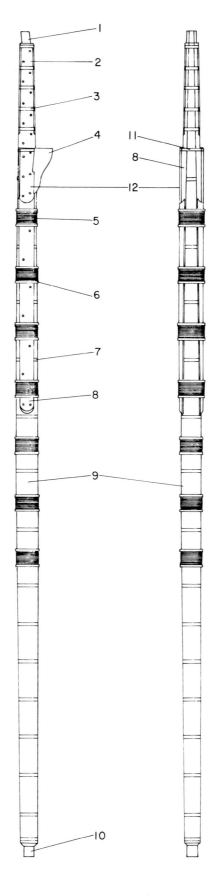

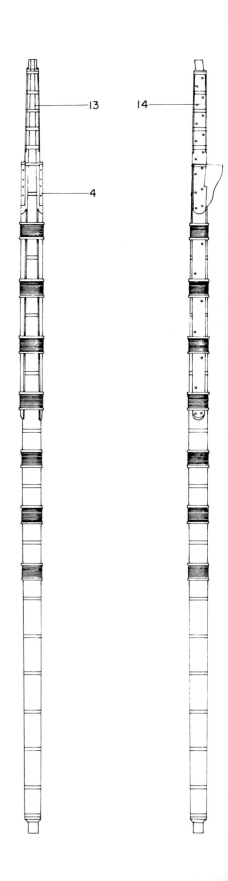

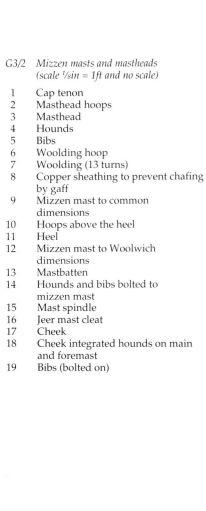

G3/2 *Mizzen masts and mastheads*
      (scale ⅛in = 1ft and no scale)

1   Cap tenon
2   Masthead hoops
3   Masthead
4   Hounds
5   Bibs
6   Woolding hoop
7   Woolding (13 turns)
8   Copper sheathing to prevent chafing
    by gaff
9   Mizzen mast to common
    dimensions
10 Hoops above the heel
11 Heel
12 Mizzen mast to Woolwich
    dimensions
13 Mastbatten
14 Hounds and bibs bolted to
    mizzen mast
15 Mast spindle
16 Jeer mast cleat
17 Cheek
18 Cheek integrated hounds on main
    and foremast
19 Bibs (bolted on)

G3/2

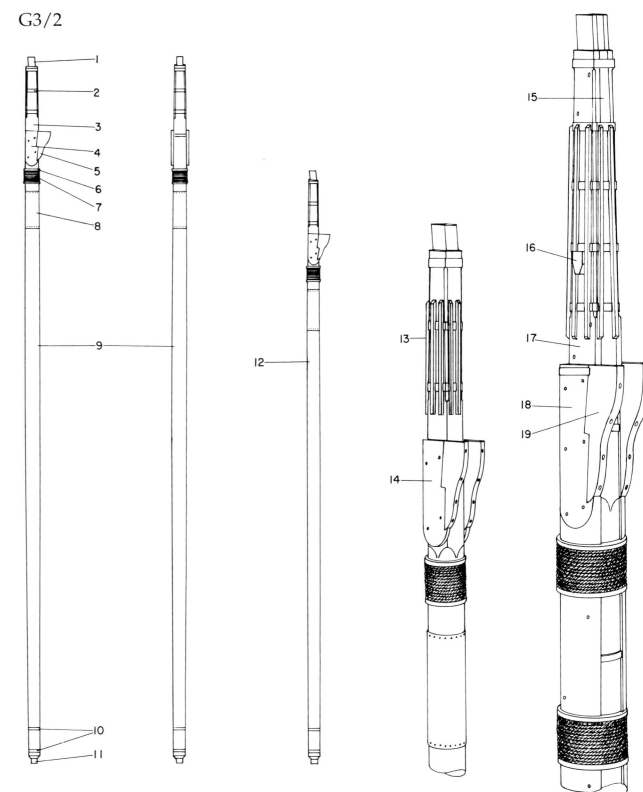

85

G Masts and yards

G3/3 *Trestle-trees, cross-trees and section
through a top (scale ¼in = 1ft)*

1   Cross-tree
2   Trestle-tree
3   Bolster
4   Middle chock
5   Fid plate
6   Deals
7   Rim
8   Batten
9   Filling
10 Gunwale

G3/4 *Lower mast caps (scale ½in = 1ft)*

1   Mainmast cap (lower side)
2   Eyebolts
3   Hole for mast tenon
4   Hole for topmast
5   Leather cuff
6   Mainmast cap (side)
7   Foremast cap (lower side)
8   Foremast cap (side)
9   Mizzenmast cap (lower side)
10 Mizzenmast cap (side)

G3/3

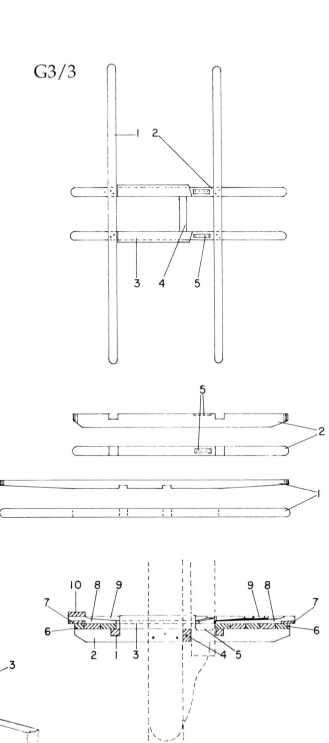

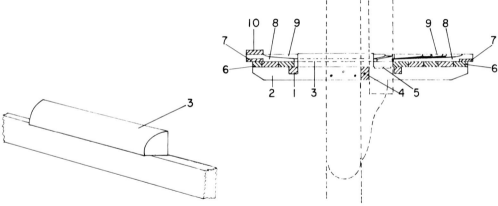

G3/4

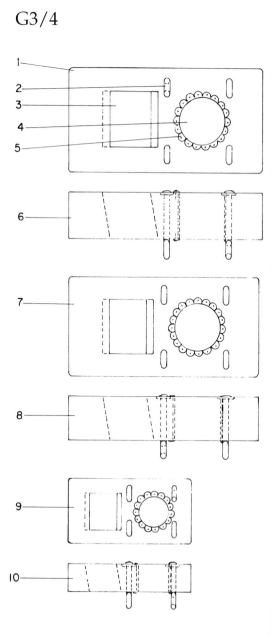

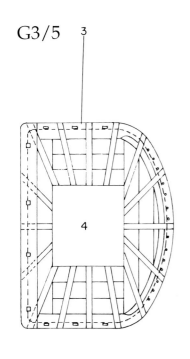

G3/5

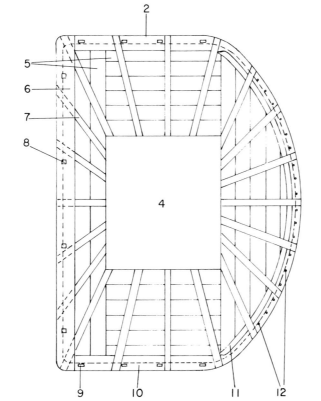

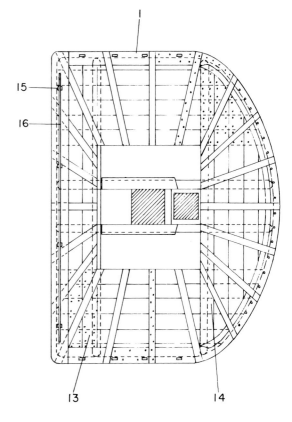

G3/5 *Mast tops (scale ¼in = 1ft)*

1 Foremast top, fitted to its trestle and
   cross-trees
2 Mainmast top
3 Mizzenmast top
4 Lubber's hole
5 Deals
6 Gunwale
7 Batten
8 Square mortises for stanchion
9 Rectangular mortises for futtocks
10 Filling between battens
11 Rim
12 14 or 18 Crowsfeet holes
13 Deal overlapping (rear)
14 Deal overlapping (front)
15 Rail stanchion
16 Rail

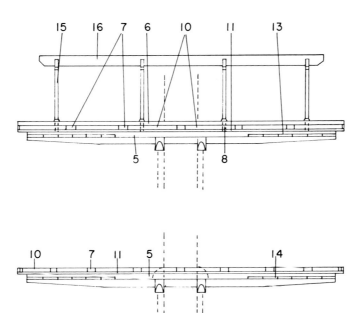

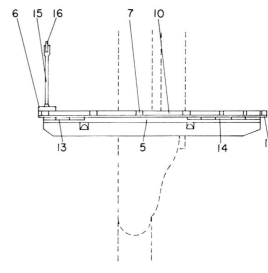

G Masts and yards

*G4/1 Topmasts and topgallant masts
(scale ⅛in = 1ft)*

G4/1

1   Fore topmast
2   Main topmast
3   Mizzen topmast
4   Fore topgallant mast
5   Main topgallant mast
6   Topmast tenon
7   Topmast-head
8   Topmast hounds
9   Upper top-rope sheave
10 Square heeling with fid hole
11 Lower top-rope sheave
12 Block
13 Block hoop
14 Truck
15 Flag line sheave
16 Long polehead
17 Sheave for mizzen top staysail
    halyard
18 Sheave for mizzen topsail yard tye
19 Sheave for topgallant top-rope
20 Square heeling with fid hole
21 Sheave for main topgallant staysail

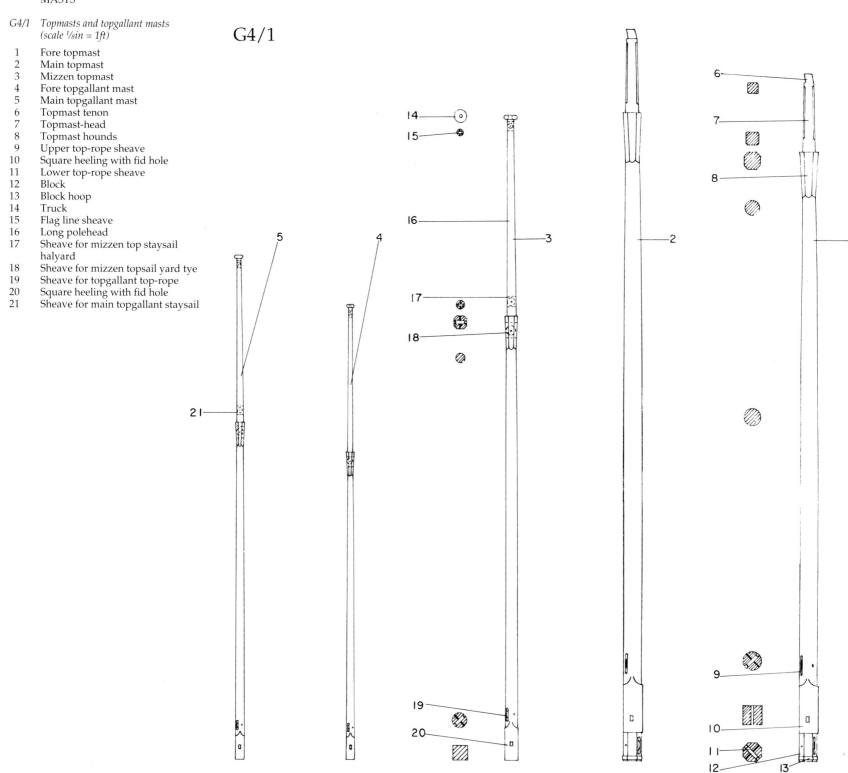

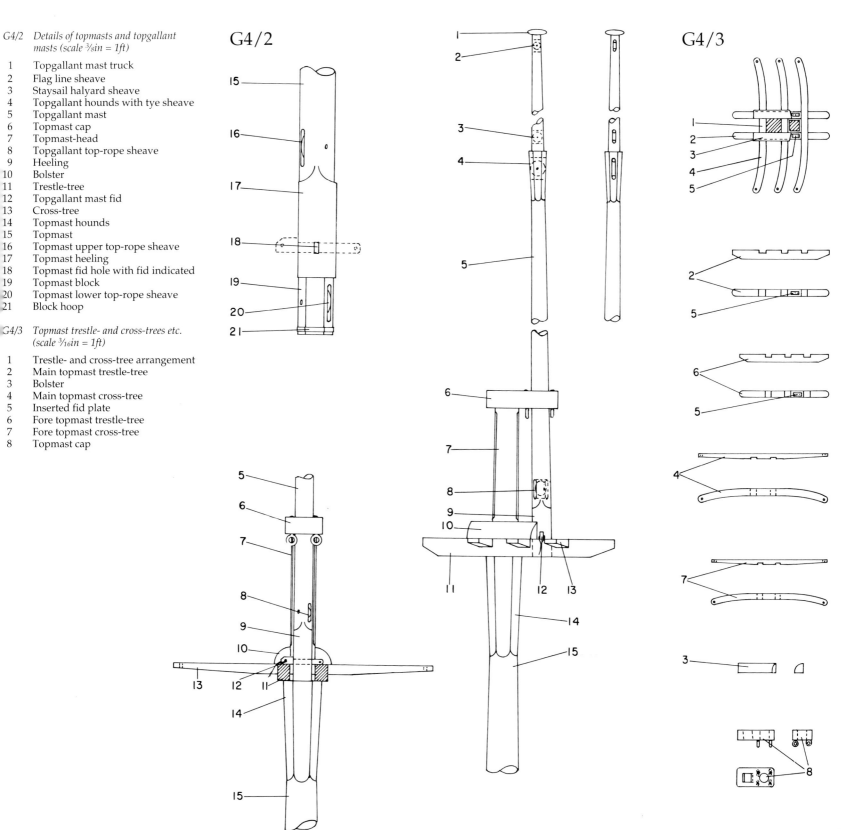

G4/2 Details of topmasts and topgallant
 masts (scale ³⁄₈in = 1ft)

1   Topgallant mast truck
2   Flag line sheave
3   Staysail halyard sheave
4   Topgallant hounds with tye sheave
5   Topgallant mast
6   Topmast cap
7   Topmast-head
8   Topgallant top-rope sheave
9   Heeling
10 Bolster
11 Trestle-tree
12 Topgallant mast fid
13 Cross-tree
14 Topmast hounds
15 Topmast
16 Topmast upper top-rope sheave
17 Topmast heeling
18 Topmast fid hole with fid indicated
19 Topmast block
20 Topmast lower top-rope sheave
21 Block hoop

G4/3 Topmast trestle- and cross-trees etc.
 (scale ³⁄₁₆in = 1ft)

1   Trestle- and cross-tree arrangement
2   Main topmast trestle-tree
3   Bolster
4   Main topmast cross-tree
5   Inserted fid plate
6   Fore topmast trestle-tree
7   Fore topmast cross-tree
8   Topmast cap

G4/2

G4/3

G Masts and yards

G5 BOWSPRIT AND JIB-BOOM
(scale ³⁄₁₆in = 1ft)

1   Bowsprit
2   Heel tenon
3   Hoop
4   Gammoning cleats
5   Fairlead saddle
6   Jib-boom saddle
7   Woolding hoop
8   Woolding (13 turns)
9   Square
10 Cap tenon
11 Bee block
12 Bee
13 Sheave for fore topmast preventer stay
14 Holes for emergency stays
15 Sheave for fore topmast stay
16 Bowsprit cap
17 Eyebolts
18 Leather clad jib-boom hole
19 Square tenon hole
20 Jackstaff channel
21 Jib-boom
22 Hole for jib-boom lashing
23 Sheave for jib-boom outhauler
24 Octagonal jib-boom heeling
25 Sheave for traveller outhauler
26 Jib-boom stop
27 Jackstaff
28 Bowsprit, jib-boom and jackstaff as fitted (²⁄₃ scale)
29 Bow with bowsprit between knightheads

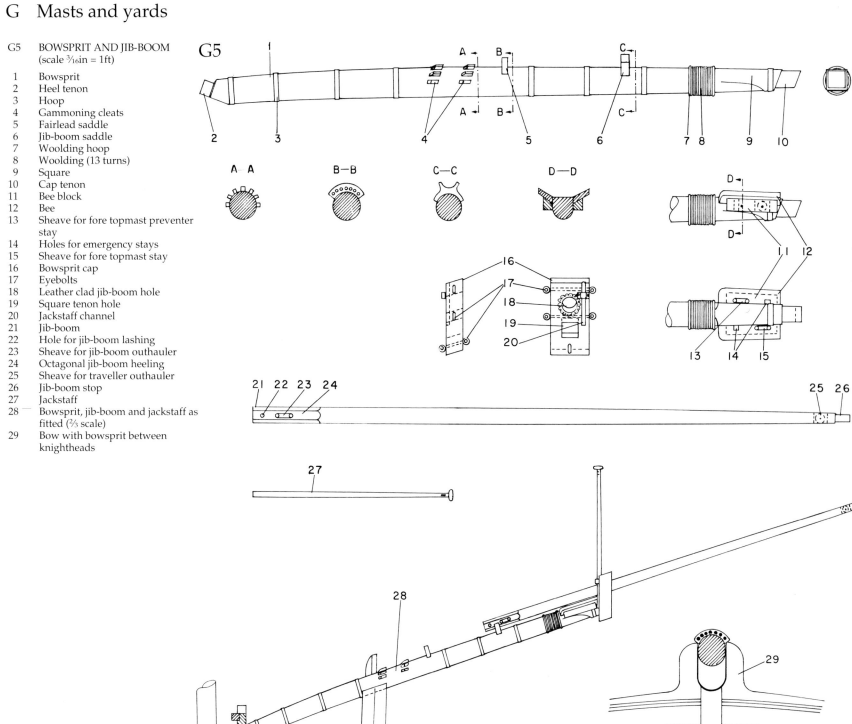

G6   YARDS (scale 3/16in = 1ft)

G6/1   *Lower yards*

1   Main yard
2   Fore yard
3   Crossjack yard
4   Octagonal centre, 7/8 are of 1/4 yard
      and 1/8 at the rear of 1/2 yard length
5   Jeer cleats
6   Topmast studdingsail boom
7   Inner boom iron
8   Yardarm stop cleat
9   Outer boom iron
10   Sling cleats
11   Sixteen-sided inner quarter
12   Ferule
13   Yard section with boom irons and
      stop cleat (no scale)
14   Inner boom iron
15   Outer boom iron as seen from end
      on

G6/1

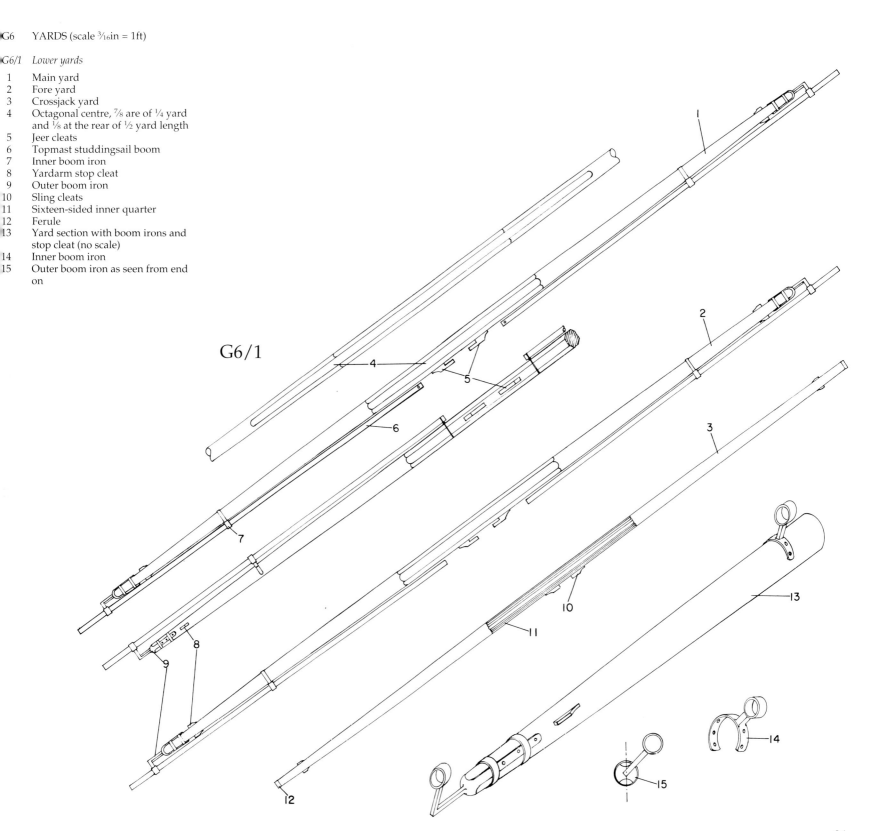

G Masts and yards

G6/2 *Topsail and topgallant yards*

1 Main topsail yard (side and plan)
2 Fore topsail yard
3 Mizzen topsail yard
4 Main topgallant yard
5 Fore topgallant yard
6 Octagonal centre, ¼ of the yard long
7 Tye cleats
8 Yardarm stop cleats
9 Yardarm sheave for reef tackle
10 Ferule
11 Ringbolt for jewel block

G6/2

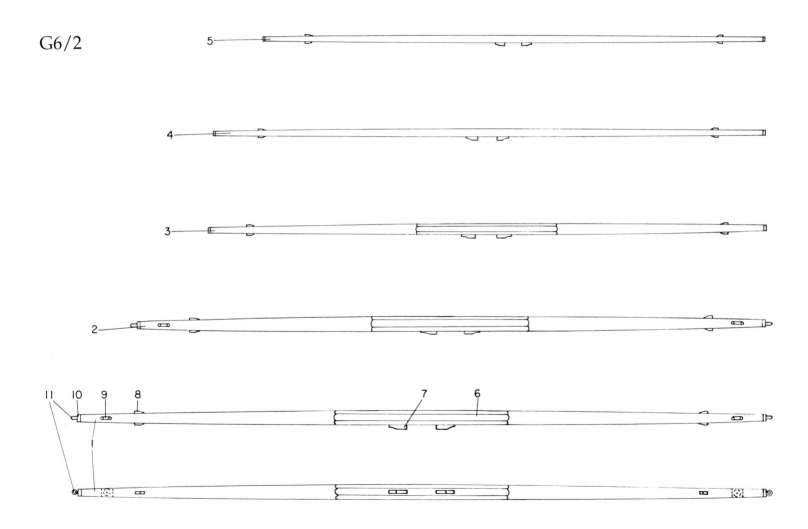

G6/3   *Spritsail and sprit-topsail yard, gaff and*
       bumpkin

1   Spritsail yard
2   Spritsail topsail yard
3   Gaff
4   Bumpkin
5   Gaff (enlarged)
6   Sling cleats
7   Yardarm stop cleats
8   Ferule
9   Eyebolt for flying signals or hoisting
    the driver
10 Peak ferule
11 Peak stop cleats
12 Cleats for peak halyard block
13 Tongue of jaws
14 Hoop
15 Eyebolt for the gaff's sling
16 Leather clad jaws
17 Eyebolt for mizzen nock
18 Hole for a single truck parrel

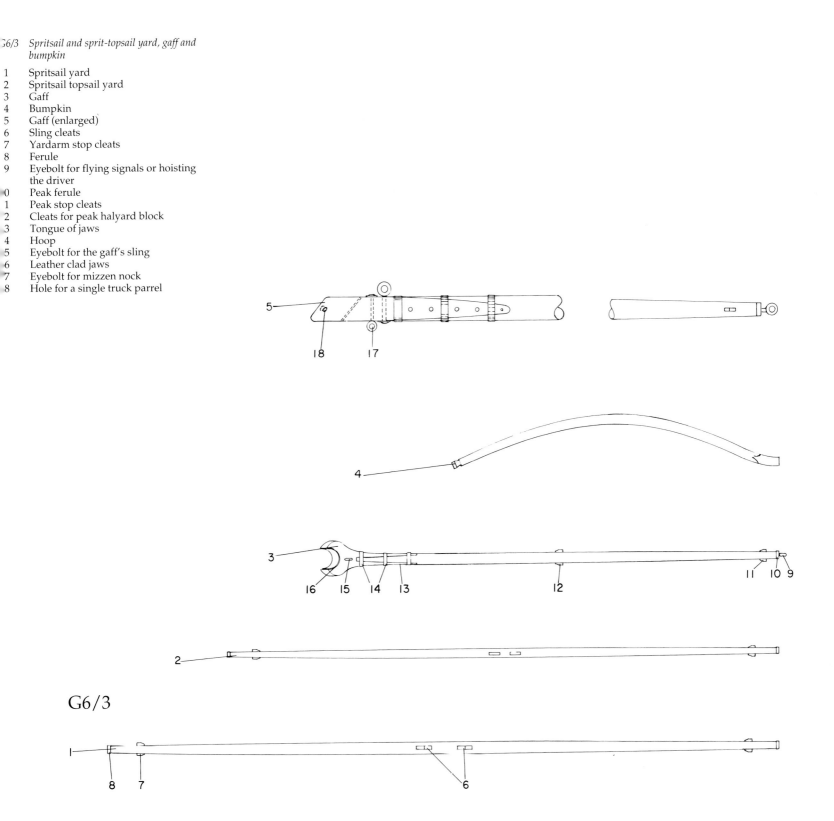

G6/3

93

G Masts and yards

G6/4

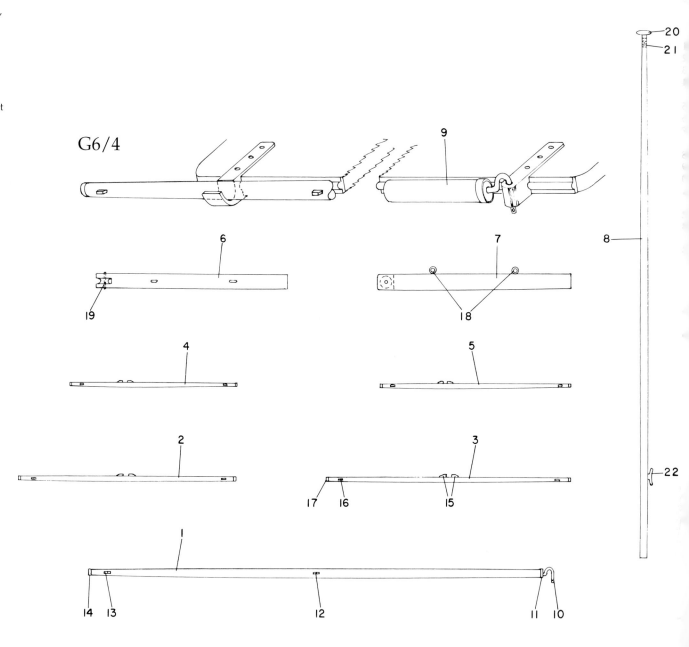

H Standing rigging

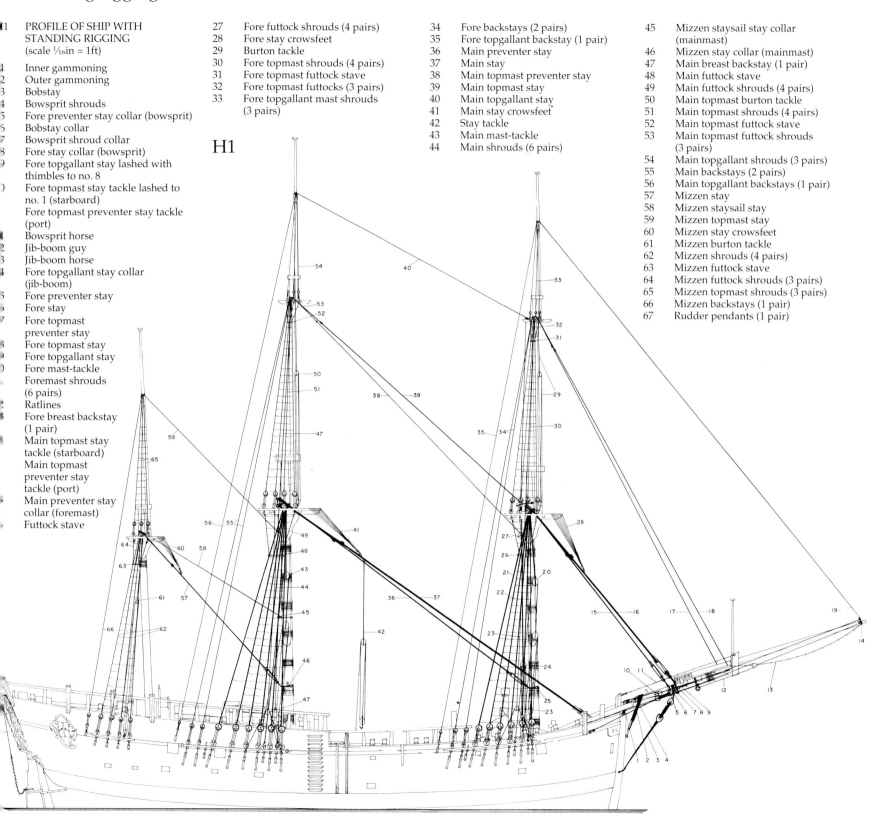

H1	PROFILE OF SHIP WITH STANDING RIGGING (scale 1/16in = 1ft)
1	Inner gammoning
2	Outer gammoning
3	Bobstay
4	Bowsprit shrouds
5	Fore preventer stay collar (bowsprit)
6	Bobstay collar
7	Bowsprit shroud collar
8	Fore stay collar (bowsprit)
9	Fore topgallant stay lashed with thimbles to no. 8
10	Fore topmast stay tackle lashed to no. 1 (starboard)
11	Fore topmast preventer stay tackle (port)
12	Bowsprit horse
13	Jib-boom guy
14	Jib-boom horse
15	Fore topgallant stay collar (jib-boom)
16	Fore preventer stay
17	Fore stay
18	Fore topmast preventer stay
19	Fore topmast stay
20	Fore topgallant stay
21	Fore mast-tackle
22	Foremast shrouds (6 pairs)
23	Ratlines
24	Fore breast backstay (1 pair)
25	Main topmast stay tackle (starboard)
26	Main topmast preventer stay tackle (port)
27	Main preventer stay collar (foremast)
28	Futtock stave

27 Fore futtock shrouds (4 pairs)
28 Fore stay crowsfeet
29 Burton tackle
30 Fore topmast shrouds (4 pairs)
31 Fore topmast futtock stave
32 Fore topmast futtocks (3 pairs)
33 Fore topgallant mast shrouds (3 pairs)

34 Fore backstays (2 pairs)
35 Fore topgallant backstay (1 pair)
36 Main preventer stay
37 Main stay
38 Main topmast preventer stay
39 Main topmast stay
40 Main topgallant stay
41 Main stay crowsfeet
42 Stay tackle
43 Main mast-tackle
44 Main shrouds (6 pairs)

45 Mizzen staysail stay collar (mainmast)
46 Mizzen stay collar (mainmast)
47 Main breast backstay (1 pair)
48 Main futtock stave
49 Main futtock shrouds (4 pairs)
50 Main topmast burton tackle
51 Main topmast shrouds (4 pairs)
52 Main topmast futtock stave
53 Main topmast futtock shrouds (3 pairs)
54 Main topgallant shrouds (3 pairs)
55 Main backstays (2 pairs)
56 Main topgallant backstays (1 pair)
57 Mizzen stay
58 Mizzen staysail stay
59 Mizzen topmast stay
60 Mizzen stay crowsfeet
61 Mizzen burton tackle
62 Mizzen shrouds (4 pairs)
63 Mizzen futtock stave
64 Mizzen futtock shrouds (3 pairs)
65 Mizzen topmast shrouds (3 pairs)
66 Mizzen backstays (1 pair)
67 Rudder pendants (1 pair)

H Standing rigging

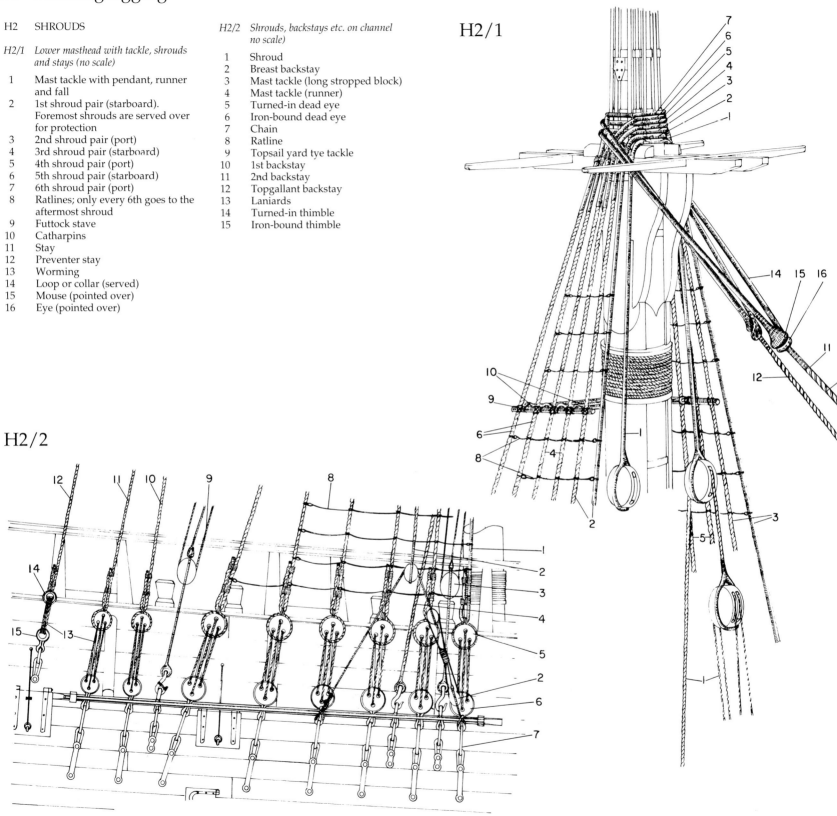

H2 SHROUDS

H2/1 Lower masthead with tackle, shrouds and stays (no scale)

1 Mast tackle with pendant, runner and fall
2 1st shroud pair (starboard). Foremost shrouds are served over for protection
3 2nd shroud pair (port)
4 3rd shroud pair (starboard)
5 4th shroud pair (port)
6 5th shroud pair (starboard)
7 6th shroud pair (port)
8 Ratlines; only every 6th goes to the aftermost shroud
9 Futtock stave
10 Catharpins
11 Stay
12 Preventer stay
13 Worming
14 Loop or collar (served)
15 Mouse (pointed over)
16 Eye (pointed over)

H2/2 Shrouds, backstays etc. on channel no scale)

1 Shroud
2 Breast backstay
3 Mast tackle (long stropped block)
4 Mast tackle (runner)
5 Turned-in dead eye
6 Iron-bound dead eye
7 Chain
8 Ratline
9 Topsail yard tye tackle
10 1st backstay
11 2nd backstay
12 Topgallant backstay
13 Laniards
14 Turned-in thimble
15 Iron-bound thimble

H2/1

H2/2

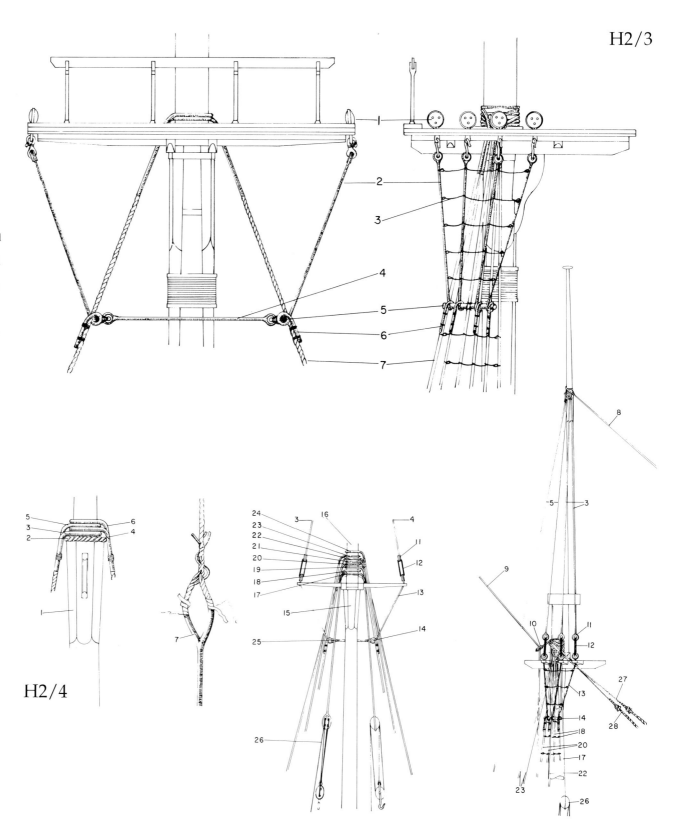

H2/3

H2/4

H   Standing rigging

H2/5   Shroud details (no scale)

1   Catharpin leg
2   Ratline, clove hitched and lashed
    with an eye at the ends
3   Futtock shroud with hook and
    thimble secured to a futtock dead
    eye
4   Turned-in dead eye with its eye,
    throat and end seizings
5   Iron-bound channel dead eye
6   Upper link
7   Middle link
8   Preventer link
9   Eye of a shroud pair with its seizing

H2/5

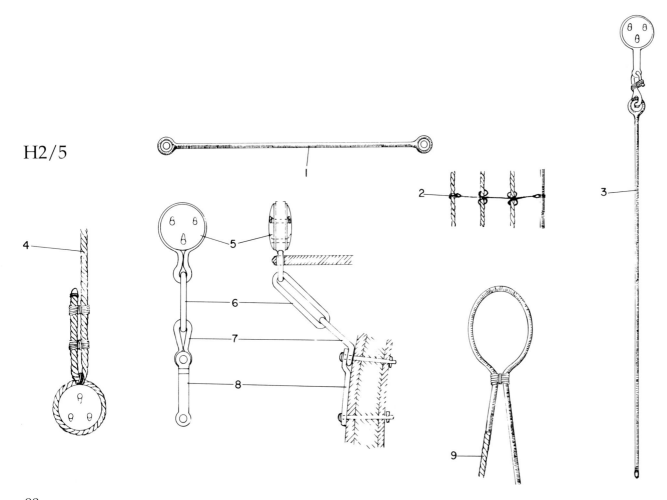

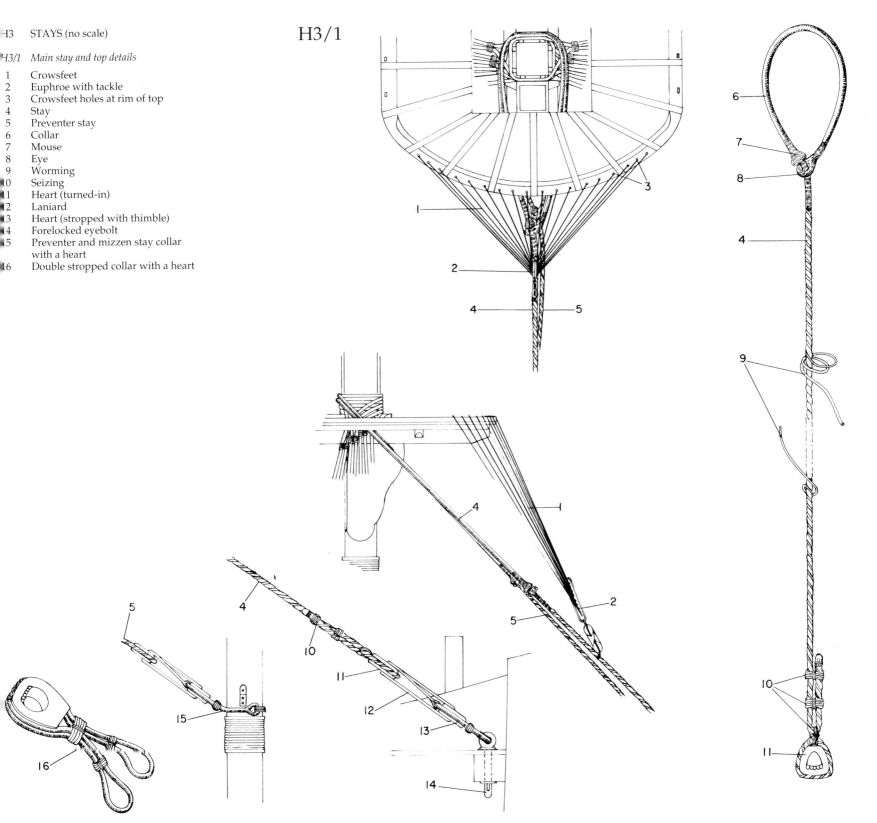

H3 STAYS (no scale)

H3/1 *Main stay and top details*

1   Crowsfeet
2   Euphroe with tackle
3   Crowsfeet holes at rim of top
4   Stay
5   Preventer stay
6   Collar
7   Mouse
8   Eye
9   Worming
10 Seizing
11 Heart (turned-in)
12 Laniard
13 Heart (stropped with thimble)
14 Forelocked eyebolt
15 Preventer and mizzen stay collar
    with a heart
16 Double stropped collar with a heart

H3/1

H Standing rigging

H3/2

H3/3

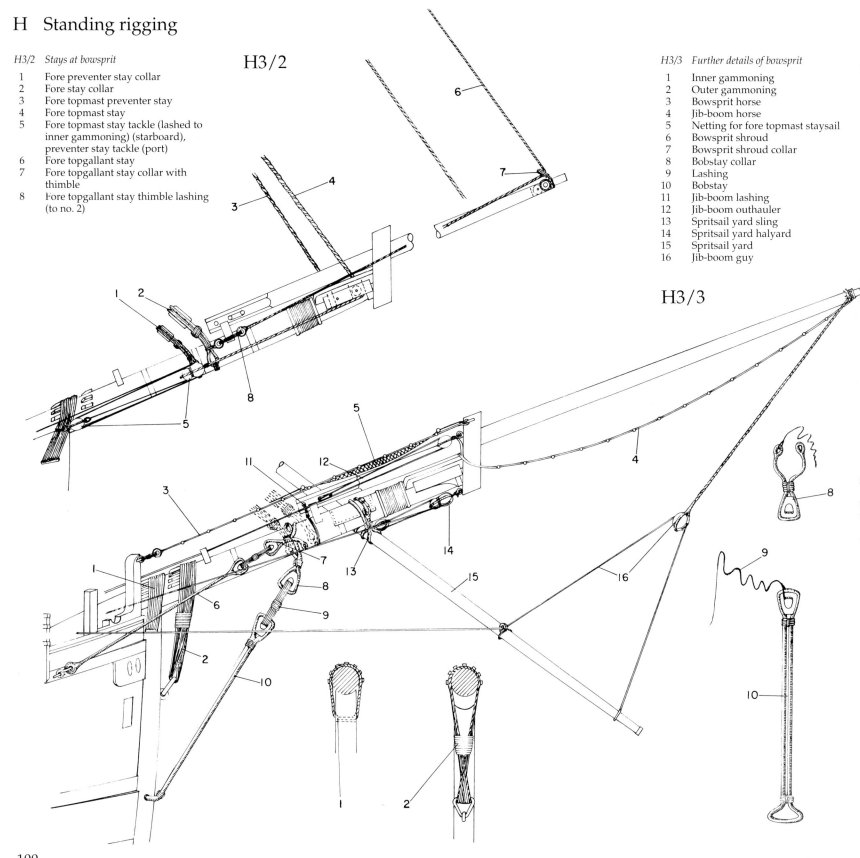

H3/4

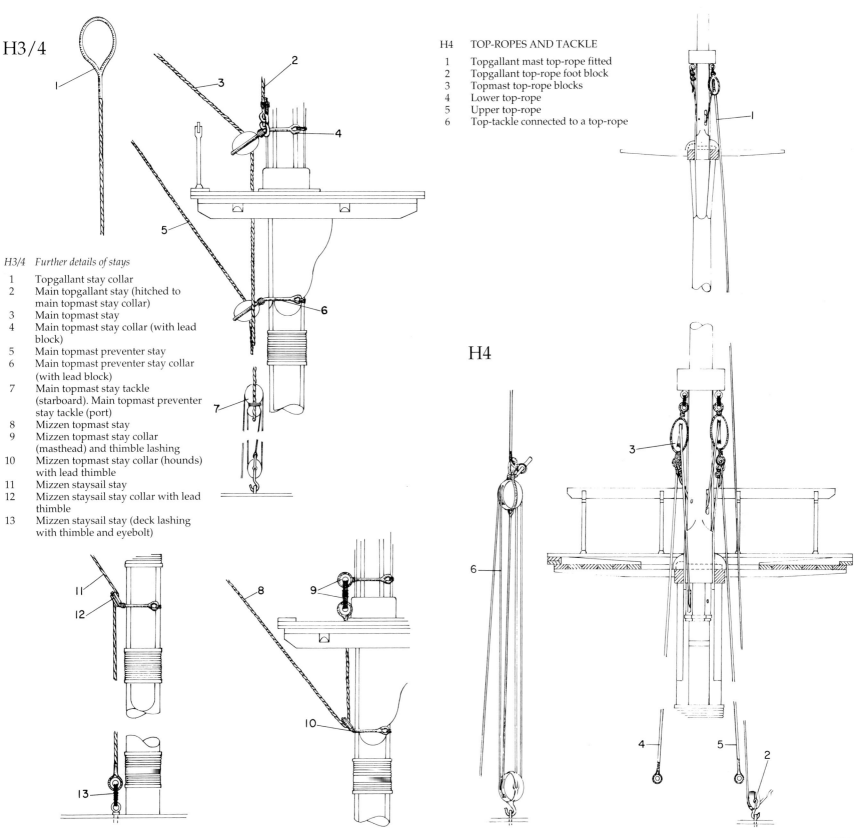

H4

101

I Running rigging

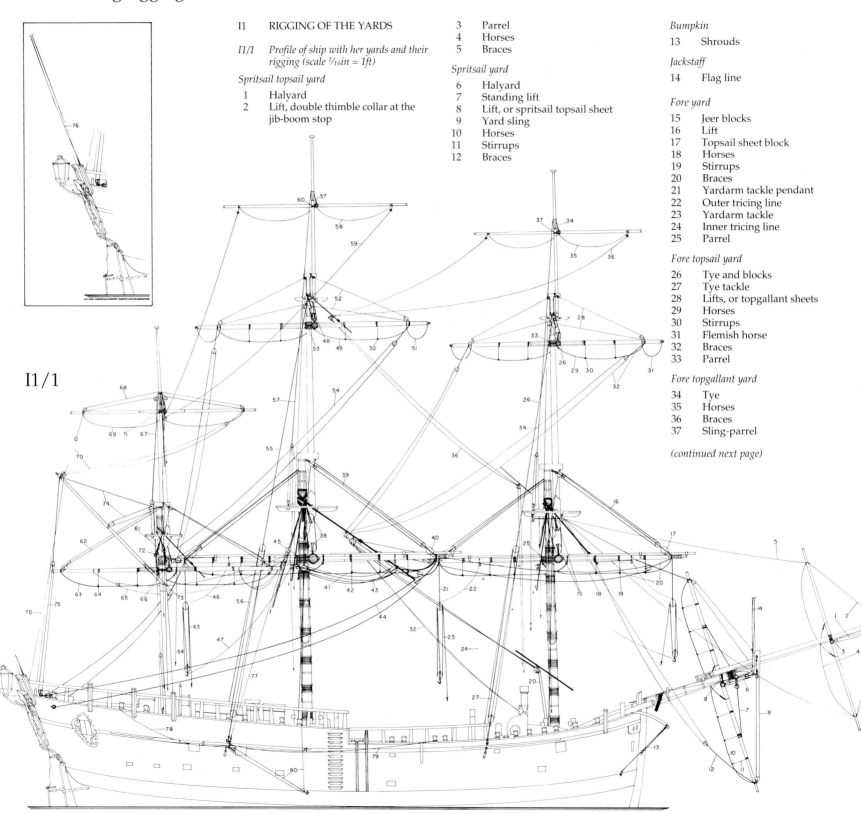

I1 RIGGING OF THE YARDS

I1/1 Profile of ship with her yards and their rigging (scale 1/16in = 1ft)

Spritsail topsail yard
1　Halyard
2　Lift, double thimble collar at the jib-boom stop

Spritsail yard
6　Halyard
7　Standing lift
8　Lift, or spritsail topsail sheet
9　Yard sling
10　Horses
11　Stirrups
12　Braces

3　Parrel
4　Horses
5　Braces

Bumpkin
13　Shrouds

Jackstaff
14　Flag line

Fore yard
15　Jeer blocks
16　Lift
17　Topsail sheet block
18　Horses
19　Stirrups
20　Braces
21　Yardarm tackle pendant
22　Outer tricing line
23　Yardarm tackle
24　Inner tricing line
25　Parrel

Fore topsail yard
26　Tye and blocks
27　Tye tackle
28　Lifts, or topgallant sheets
29　Horses
30　Stirrups
31　Flemish horse
32　Braces
33　Parrel

Fore topgallant yard
34　Tye
35　Horses
36　Braces
37　Sling-parrel

(continued next page)

I1/1

Main yard

38	Jeer blocks
39	Lift
40	Topsail sheet block
41	Horses
42	Stirrups
43	Yardarm tackle
44	Braces
45	Parrel
46	Outer tricing line
47	Inner tricing line

Main topsail yard

48	Tye block
49	Horses
50	Stirrups
51	Flemish horse
52	Lift, or topgallant sheet
53	Parrel
54	Braces
55	Tye
56	Tye tackle

Main topgallant yard

57	Tye
58	Horses
59	Braces
60	Sling-parrel

Crossjack yard

61	Yard slings
62	Lift
63	Horses
64	Stirrups
65	Braces
66	Truss

Mizzen topsail yard

67	Tye
68	Lift
69	Horses
70	Braces
71	Parrel

Gaff

72	Slings
73	Parrel
74	Peak halyard
75	Vangs

Ensign staff

| 76 | Flag line |

Main lower studdingsail boom

77	Lift
78	After guy
79	Forward guy
80	Martingale

I1/2   Lower yards (no scale)

1	Jeer double blocks (double stropped yard blocks)
2	Jeer double blocks (double stropped mast blocks)
3	Masthead jeer block cleat
4	Jeers
5	Jeer mast block lashing
6	Fiddle block (stropped with thimble)
7	Lift block and topsail sheet block (stropped together)
8	Lift
9	Standing part of the lift spliced around a yardarm thimble strop
10	Brace pendant with spliced in block
11	Yardarm tackle pendant
12	Outer tricing line
13	Horses
14	Stirrups; served over and the end plaited, goes 2½ times around the yard and is nailed to it
15	Leech line and lead blocks
16	Buntlines and lead blocks
17	Clew-garnet and yard block
18	Quarter block (topsail sheet lead block) with a slabline block stropped underneath
19	Spritsail yard brace
20	Spritsail topsail yard brace
21	Parrel

I1/2

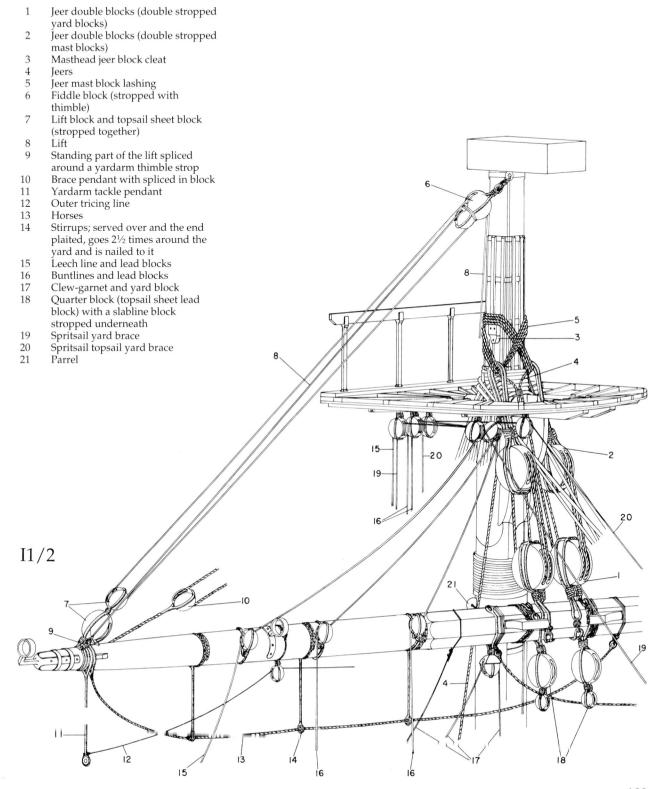

I Running rigging

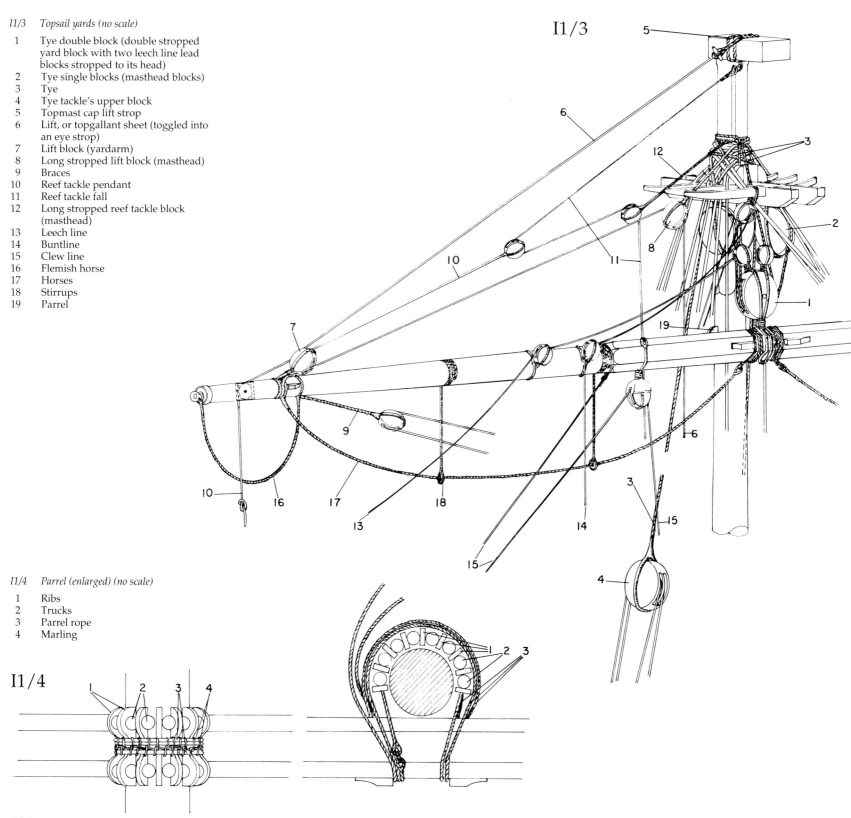

I1/3 Topsail yards (no scale)

1 Tye double block (double stropped yard block with two leech line lead blocks stropped to its head)
2 Tye single blocks (masthead blocks)
3 Tye
4 Tye tackle's upper block
5 Topmast cap lift strop
6 Lift, or topgallant sheet (toggled into an eye strop)
7 Lift block (yardarm)
8 Long stropped lift block (masthead)
9 Braces
10 Reef tackle pendant
11 Reef tackle fall
12 Long stropped reef tackle block (masthead)
13 Leech line
14 Buntline
15 Clew line
16 Flemish horse
17 Horses
18 Stirrups
19 Parrel

I1/3

I1/4 Parrel (enlarged) (no scale)

1 Ribs
2 Trucks
3 Parrel rope
4 Marling

I1/4

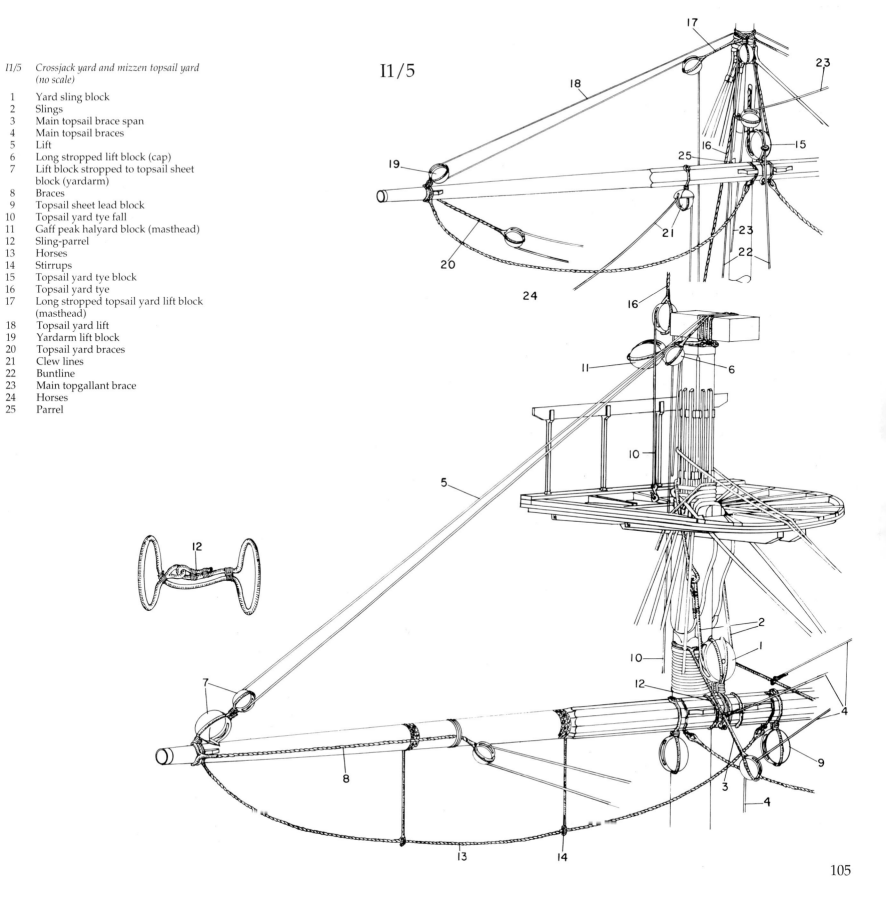

I1/5 *Crossjack yard and mizzen topsail yard*
      (no scale)

I1/5

1   Yard sling block
2   Slings
3   Main topsail brace span
4   Main topsail braces
5   Lift
6   Long stropped lift block (cap)
7   Lift block stropped to topsail sheet
     block (yardarm)
8   Braces
9   Topsail sheet lead block
10   Topsail yard tye fall
11   Gaff peak halyard block (masthead)
12   Sling-parrel
13   Horses
14   Stirrups
15   Topsail yard tye block
16   Topsail yard tye
17   Long stropped topsail yard lift block
     (masthead)
18   Topsail yard lift
19   Yardarm lift block
20   Topsail yard braces
21   Clew lines
22   Buntline
23   Main topgallant brace
24   Horses
25   Parrel

I   Running rigging

I1/6   Topgallant yard (no scale)

1   Tye
2   Braces (toggled)
3   Horses
4   Sling-parrel

I1/7   Gaff (no scale)

1   Slings
2   Peak halyard
3   Vangs
4   Throat brails
5   Middle brails
6   Peak brails
7   Fancy line
8   Mizzen topsail yard braces, stand-
     ing part fastened to the gaff's peak
9   Parrel

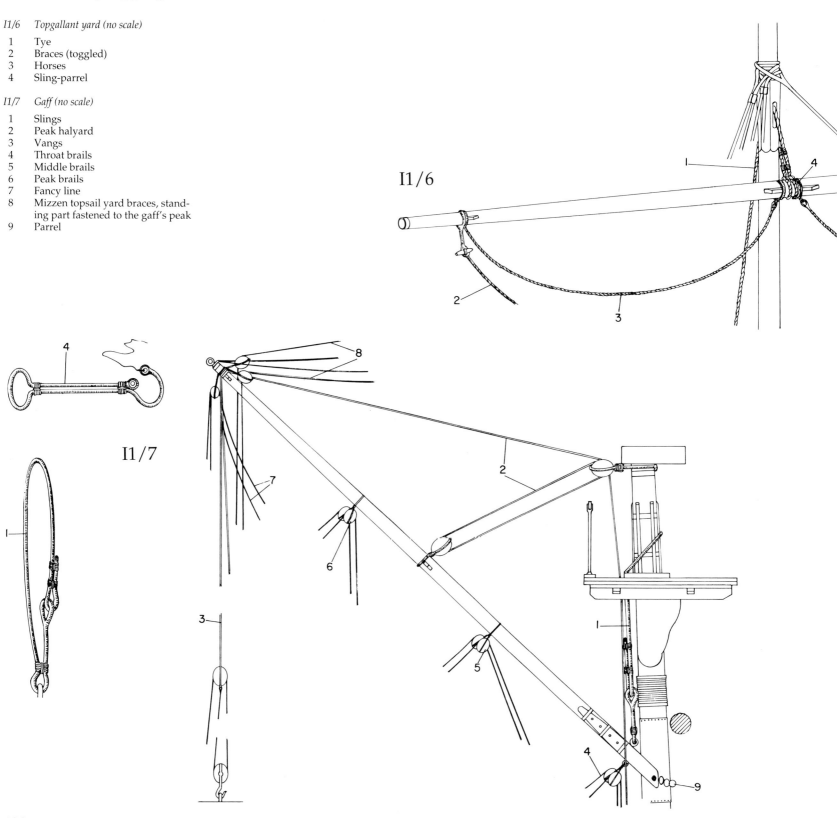

I1/6

I1/7

I1/8

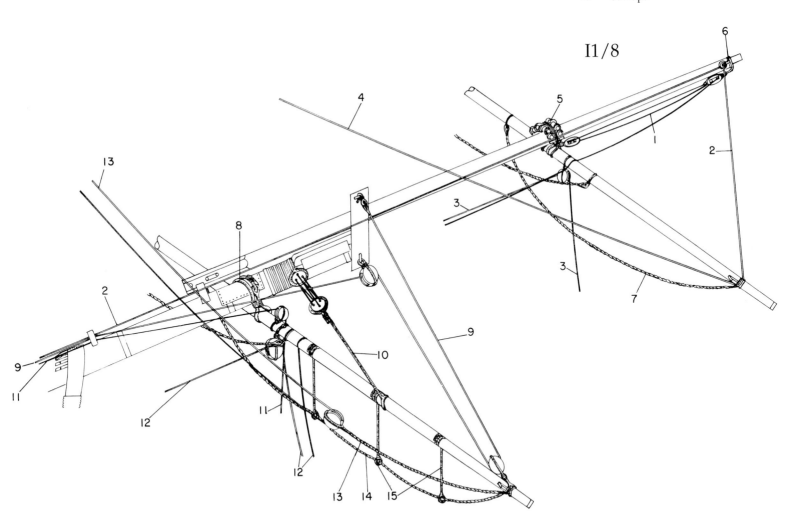

I Running rigging

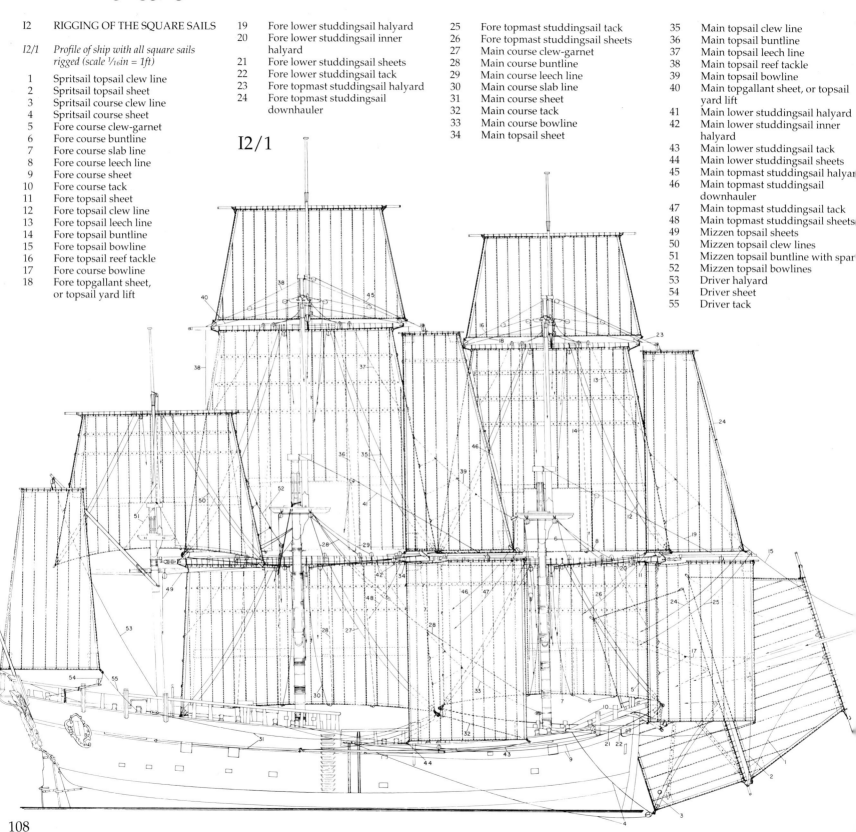

I2/1

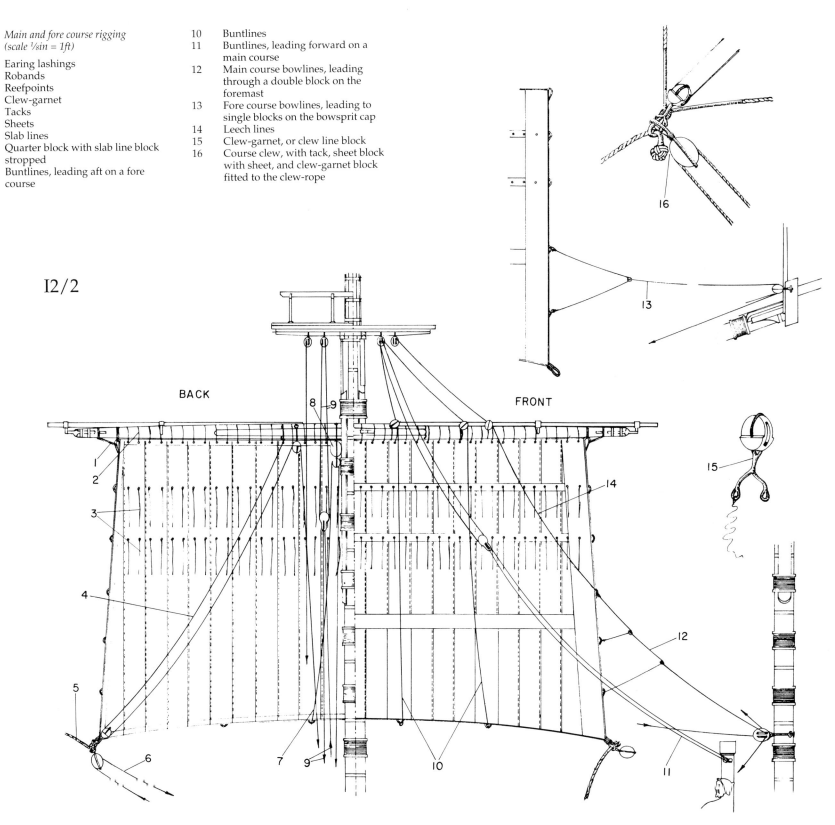

I2/2 Main and fore course rigging
(scale 1/8in = 1ft)

1 Earing lashings
2 Robands
3 Reefpoints
4 Clew-garnet
5 Tacks
6 Sheets
7 Slab lines
8 Quarter block with slab line block stropped
9 Buntlines, leading aft on a fore course
10 Buntlines
11 Buntlines, leading forward on a main course
12 Main course bowlines, leading through a double block on the foremast
13 Fore course bowlines, leading to single blocks on the bowsprit cap
14 Leech lines
15 Clew-garnet, or clew line block
16 Course clew, with tack, sheet block with sheet, and clew-garnet block fitted to the clew-rope

I2/2

BACK

FRONT

I Running rigging

I2/3 *Topsail and topgallant sail rigging*
(scale ⅛in = 1ft)

1   Earing lashings
2   Robands
3   Reefpoints
4   Clew line
5   Topsail sheet block with lift block
    stropped
6   Sheet
7   Buntline
8   Leech line
9   Reef tackle
10 Main topsail bowlines
11 Fore topsail bowlines
12 Topgallant sheet
13 Eye strop around cap to take the
    toggle of no. 12 if the topgallant sail
    is not hoisted
14 Topgallant sheet toggled to the sail's
    clew
15 Fore topgallant stay and fore
    topsail bowlines strop.
    Spritsail topsail lift strop
    is similar but has only
    two thimbles

I2/3

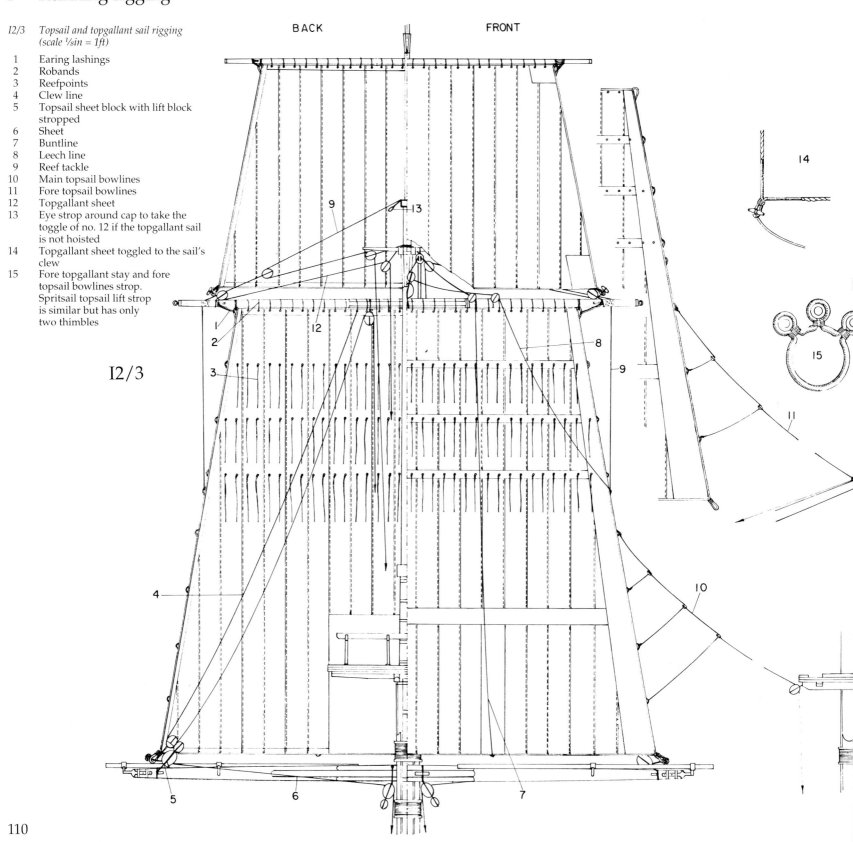

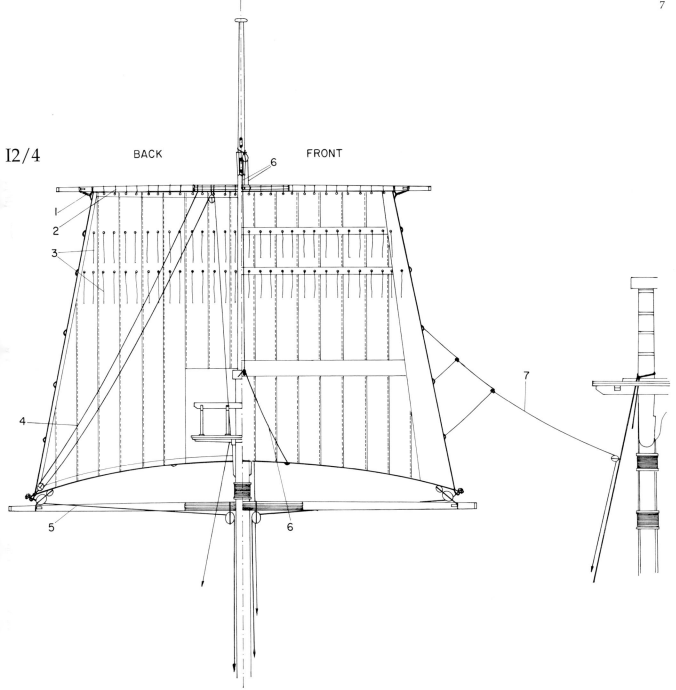

I2/4   *Mizzen topsail rigging*
(*scale ¹⁄₈in = 1ft*)

1   Earing lashings
2   Robands
3   Reefpoints
4   Clew lines
5   Sheets
6   Buntline with a span
7   Bowlines

BACK

FRONT

I Running rigging

I2/5 *Spritsail topsail and spritsail course rigging (scale ⅛in = 1ft)*

1 Earing lashings
2 Robands
3 Clew line
4 Spritsail topsail sheet or spritsail yard lift
5 Reefpoints
6 Clew line
7 Spritsail course sheets
8 Buntline

I2/5

BACK   FRONT

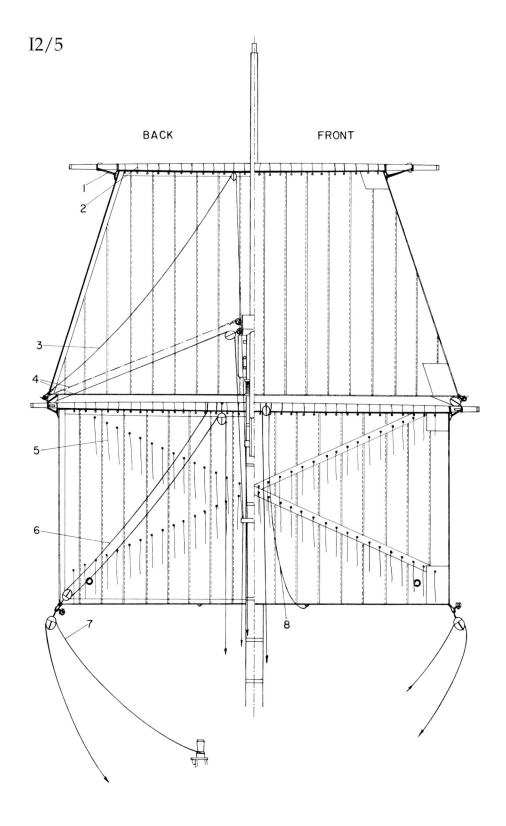

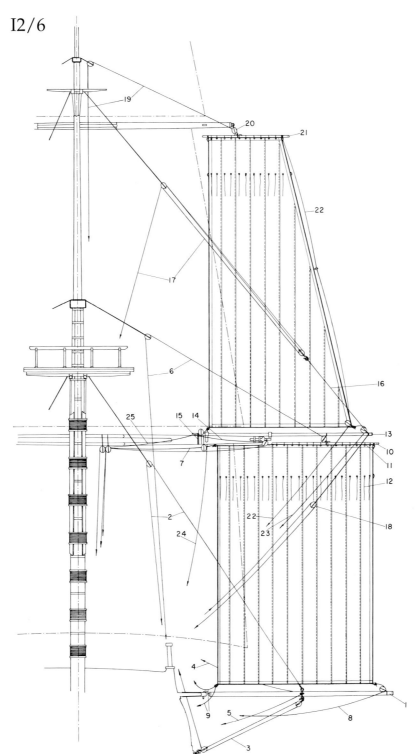

I2/6

I2/7

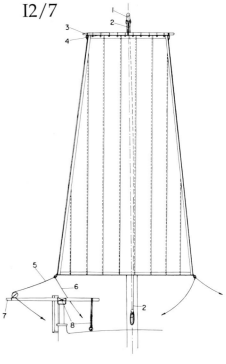

I Running rigging

I2/8 Various block fittings (no scale)

1 A long tackle
2 Fiddle, or long tackle block, often used instead of the double block on a long tackle
3 Stropped single block with a tail
4 Stropped single block with an eye
5 Stropped single block with a short and a long leg
6 Stropped single block with hook and thimble
7 Double stropped double block
8 Iron-bound block with hook
9 Iron-bound block with swivel hook
10 Cat block
11 Shoe block
12 Stropped topsail sheet and lift blocks
13 Stropped sprit course sheet block with a spritsail sheet knot
14 Stropped clew line or clew-garnet block
15 Snatch block with stropping hole

I3 RIGGING OF THE FORE AND AFT SAILS

I3/1 Profile of ship with fore and aft sails rigged (scale 1/16in = 1ft)

1 Jib (hoisted flying)
2 Halyard
3 Tack (lashed to traveller)
4 Traveller
5 Traveller outhauler
6 Sheets
7 Fore topmast staysail (hoisted on fore topmast preventer stay)
8 Halyard
9 Wooden hanks
10 Tack (lashed to eyebolt in bees)
11 Downhauler
12 Sheets
13 Main staysail (hoisted on main preventer stay)
14 Halyard
15 Wooden hanks
16 Tack (lashed to main preventer stay collar)
17 Downhauler
18 Sheets
19 Main topmast staysail (hoisted on main topmast preventer stay)
20 Clew lifter and downhauler
21 Brails
22 Halyard
23 Wooden hanks
24 Nock (lashed to eyebolt of main topmast preventer stay lead block)
25 Double tack (leads through fairlead trucks on fore shroud)
26 Sheets
27 Main topgallant staysail (hoisted on main topgallant stay)
28 Halyard
29 Wooden hanks
30 Downhauler
31 Nock (lashed to main topgallant stay collar)
32 Double tack (leads through fairlead trucks on main topmast shrouds)
33 Sheets
34 Mizzen staysail (hoisted on mizzen staysail stay)
35 Halyard
36 Wooden hanks
37 Downhauler
38 Nock (lashed to mizzen staysail stay collar)
39 Tack (lashed to eyebolt on deck)
40 Clew lifting brails
41 Sheet (hooked to an eyebolt at the weather side)
42 Mizzen topmast staysail (hoisted on mizzen topmast stay)
43 Halyard
44 Wooden hanks
45 Downhauler
46 Nock (lashed to eyebolt of mizzen topmast stay lead truck)

I2/8

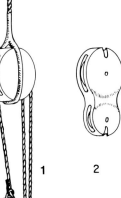

1

2

3

4

5

6

7

8

9

10

11

12

13

14

15

7 Double tack (leads through fairlead
  trucks on main shrouds)
8 Sheets
9 Mizzen (laced to gaff and mizzen
  mast)
0 Peak earing (lashed to gaff peak
  stop)
1 Head lacing
2 Nock earing (lashed to eyebolt in
  gaff jaws)
3 Bunt lacing
4 Tack (lashed to an eyebolt on deck)
5 Reef points or knittles
9 Peak brails
8 Middle brails
9 Throat brails
0 Fancy-line
0 Sheet (on iron horse)

3/1

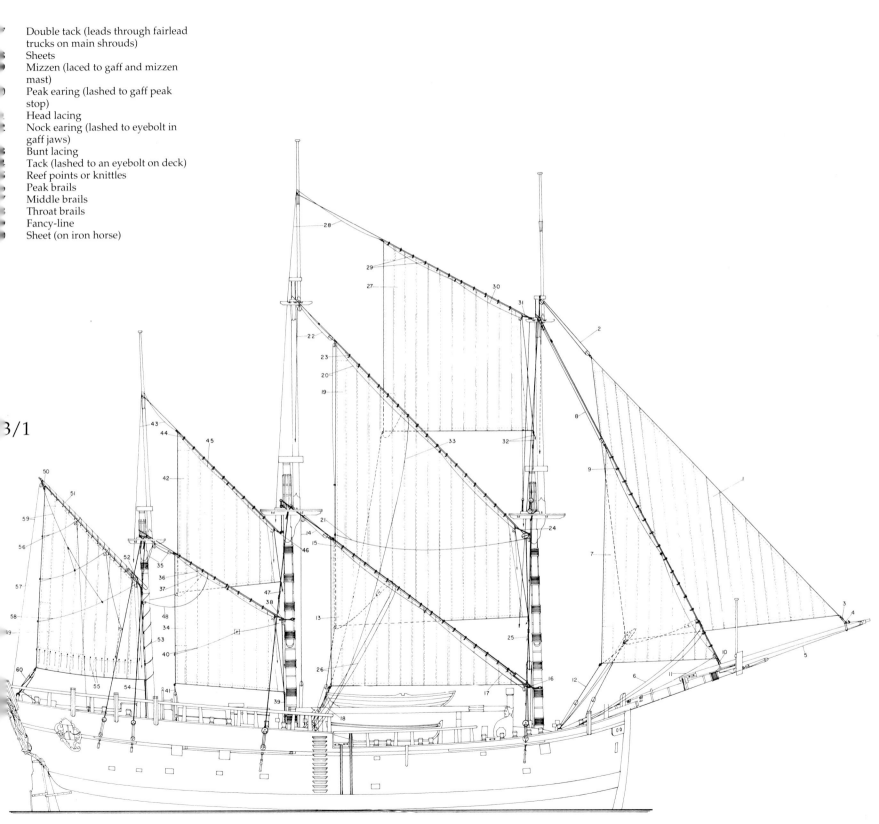

115

I Running rigging

I3/2 Headsail rigging (no scale)

1   Jib
2   Halyard
3   Tack lashed to traveller
4   Leather clad traveller
5   Traveller outhauler
6   Sheets (standing part fixed to
    eyebolt on deck, running part
    belayed to timberhead)
7   Fore topmast staysail
8   Fore topmast preventer stay
9   Wooden hanks
10 Tack, lashed to eyebolt in the bees
11 Downhauler
12 Halyard

I3/2

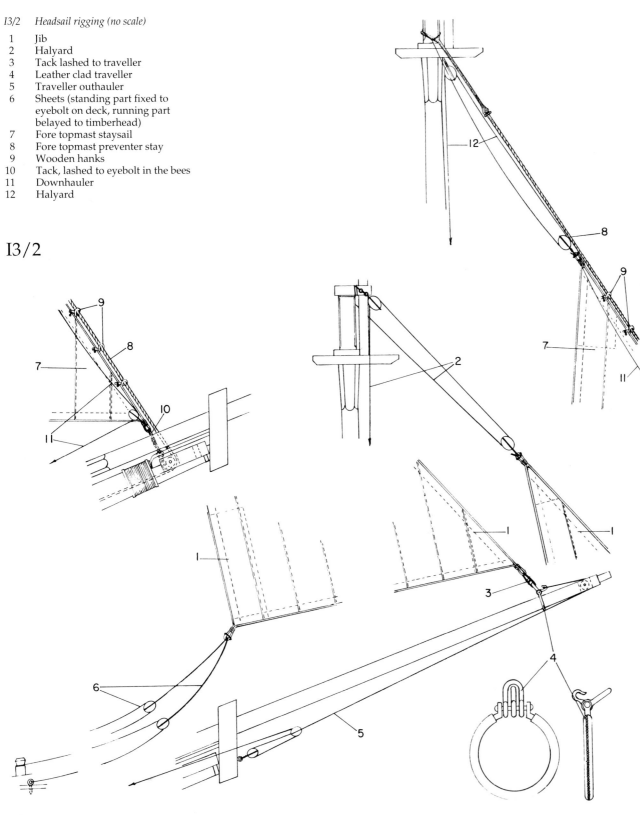

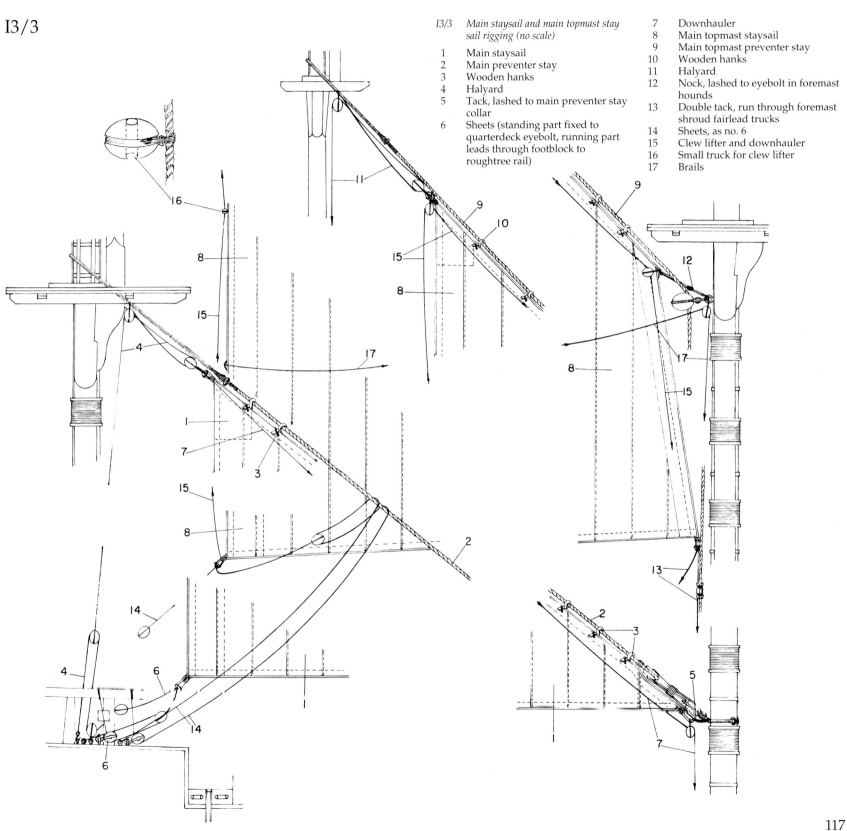

I3/3

I   Running rigging

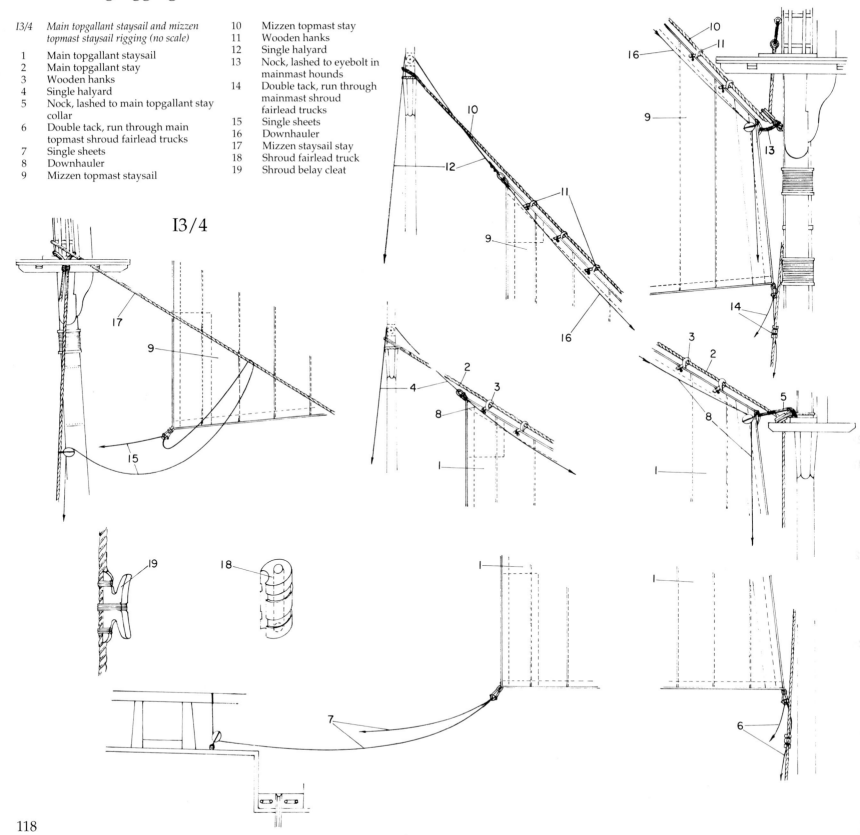

I3/4   *Main topgallant staysail and mizzen*
        topmast staysail rigging (no scale)

1   Main topgallant staysail
2   Main topgallant stay
3   Wooden hanks
4   Single halyard
5   Nock, lashed to main topgallant stay
     collar
6   Double tack, run through main
     topmast shroud fairlead trucks
7   Single sheets
8   Downhauler
9   Mizzen topmast staysail

10   Mizzen topmast stay
11   Wooden hanks
12   Single halyard
13   Nock, lashed to eyebolt in
      mainmast hounds
14   Double tack, run through
      mainmast shroud
      fairlead trucks
15   Single sheets
16   Downhauler
17   Mizzen staysail stay
18   Shroud fairlead truck
19   Shroud belay cleat

I3/4

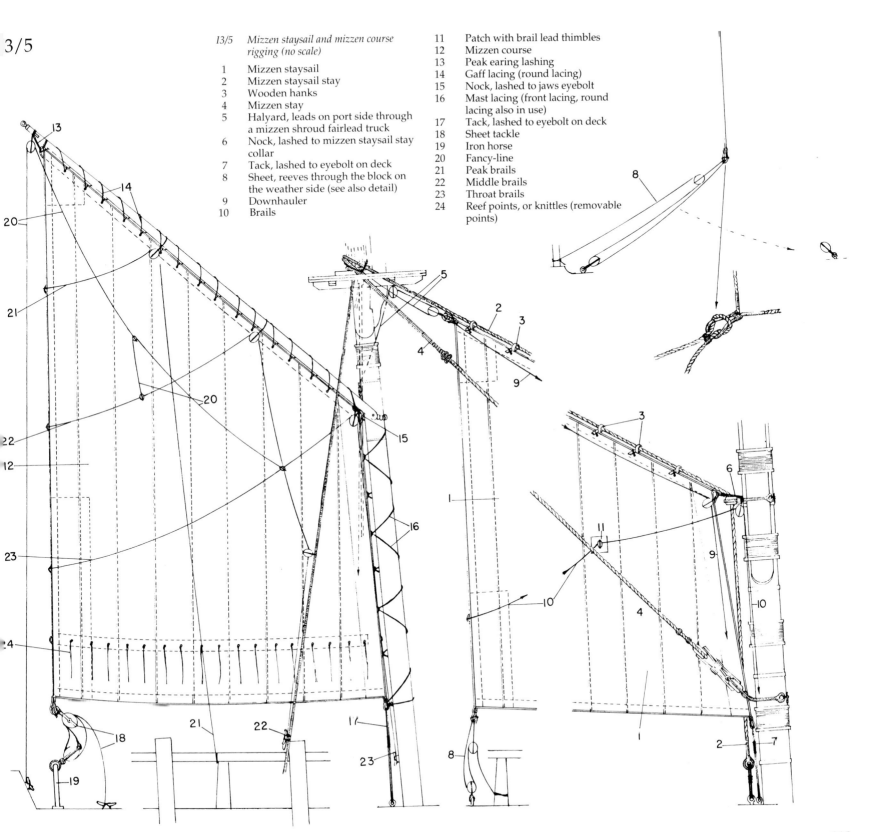

13/5 *Mizzen staysail and mizzen course*
rigging (no scale)

1   Mizzen staysail
2   Mizzen staysail stay
3   Wooden hanks
4   Mizzen stay
5   Halyard, leads on port side through
    a mizzen shroud fairlead truck
6   Nock, lashed to mizzen staysail stay
    collar
7   Tack, lashed to eyebolt on deck
8   Sheet, reeves through the block on
    the weather side (see also detail)
9   Downhauler
10 Brails

11 Patch with brail lead thimbles
12 Mizzen course
13 Peak earing lashing
14 Gaff lacing (round lacing)
15 Nock, lashed to jaws eyebolt
16 Mast lacing (front lacing, round
    lacing also in use)
17 Tack, lashed to eyebolt on deck
18 Sheet tackle
19 Iron horse
20 Fancy-line
21 Peak brails
22 Middle brails
23 Throat brails
24 Reef points, or knittles (removable
    points)

I   Running rigging

I4   BELAYING POSITIONS
      (scale ⅛in = 1ft)

I4/1   *Plan*

I4/2   *Profile*

A   Bowsprit
B   Fore topsail sheet bits
C   Foremast
D   Fore jeer bits
E   Windlass crosspiece
F   Belfry
G   Timberheads
H   Main topsail sheet bits
I   Mainmast
J   Main jeer bits
K   Mizzenmast
L   Taffarel

Bowsprit

1   Jib-boom guy
2   Traveller outhauler

Spritsail topsail

3   Halyard
4   Lifts
5   Clew lines
6   Braces

Spritsail course

7   Halyard
8   Lifts
9   Clew lines
10   Buntline
11   Braces
12   Sheets

Jib

13   Halyard
14   Sheets

Fore topmast staysail

15   Halyard
16   Sheets
17   Downhauler

Fore course

18   Jeers
19   Clew-garnets
20   Buntlines
21   Leechlines
22   Lifts
23   Sheets
24   Tacks
25   Bowlines
26   Braces
27   Inner tricing-line
28   Outer tricing-line
29   Slab line
30   Mast tackle

Fore topsail

31   Tye
32   Lifts
33   Clew lines

34   Buntlines
35   Leechlines
36   Bowlines
37   Sheets
38   Braces
39   Reef tackle, belayed at the top

Fore topgallant sail

40   Braces
41   Halyard
42   Main topmast stay
43   Main topmast preventer stay

Main staysail

44   Halyard
45   Downhauler
46   Sheets

Main topmast staysail

47   Halyard
48   Downhauler
49   Brails
50   Sheets

Main topgallant staysail

51   Halyard
52   Downhauler
53   Sheets

Main course

54   Jeers
55   Clew-garnets
56   Buntlines
57   Leechlines
58   Lifts
59   Sheets
60   Tacks
61   Bowlines
62   Braces
63&64   Tricing lines
65   Slab line
66   Mast tackle

Main topsail

67   Tye
68   Lifts
69   Clew lines
70   Buntlines
71   Leechlines
72   Bowlines
73   Sheets
74   Braces
75   Reef tackle, belayed at the top

Main topgallant sail

76   Braces
77   Halyard
78   Mizzen staysail stay

Mizzen staysail

79   Halyard
80   Downhauler
81   Brails
82   Sheets

Mizzen topmast staysail

83   Halyard
84   Downhauler
85   Sheets

Crossjack yard

86   Lifts
87   Braces

Mizzen course

88   Peak halyard
89   Vangs
90   Peak brails
91   Middle brails
92   Throat brails
93   Fancy-line
94   Tack
95   Sheet

I4/1

I4/2

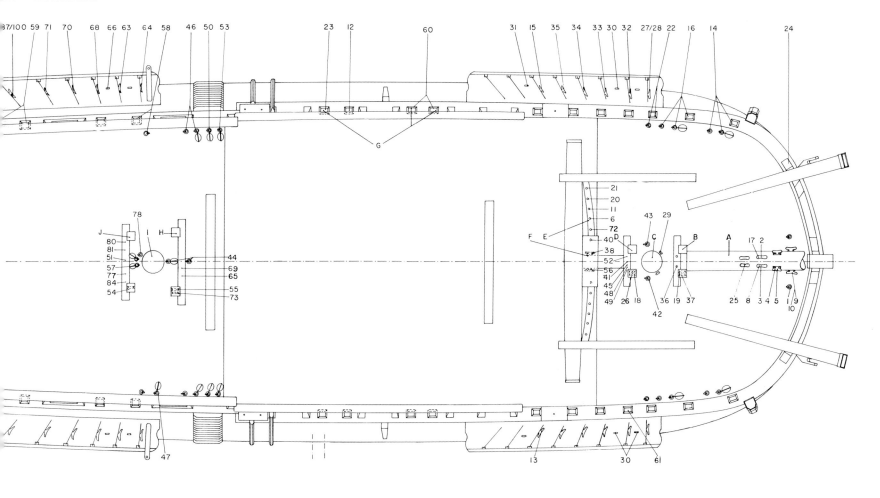

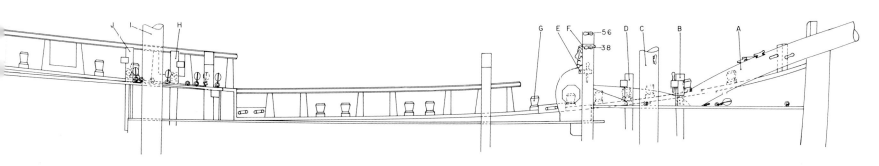

J   Sails

J1   SAIL PLAN (scale ¹⁄₁₆in = 1ft)

Fore and aft sails

1   Jib
2   Fore topmast staysail
3   Main staysail
4   Main topmast staysail
5   Main topgallant staysail
6   Mizzen staysail
7   Mizzen topmast staysail
8   Mizzen course

Square sails

9   Spritsail topsail
10   Sprit course
11   Fore course (probably two reef bands)
12   Fore topsail
13   Fore topgallant sail
14   Main course (probably two reef bands)
15   Main topsail
16   Main topgallant sail
17   Mizzen topsail

Studding sails

18   Fore lower studding sail
19   Fore topmast studding sail
20   Main lower studding sail
21   Main topmast studding sail
22   Driver

J1

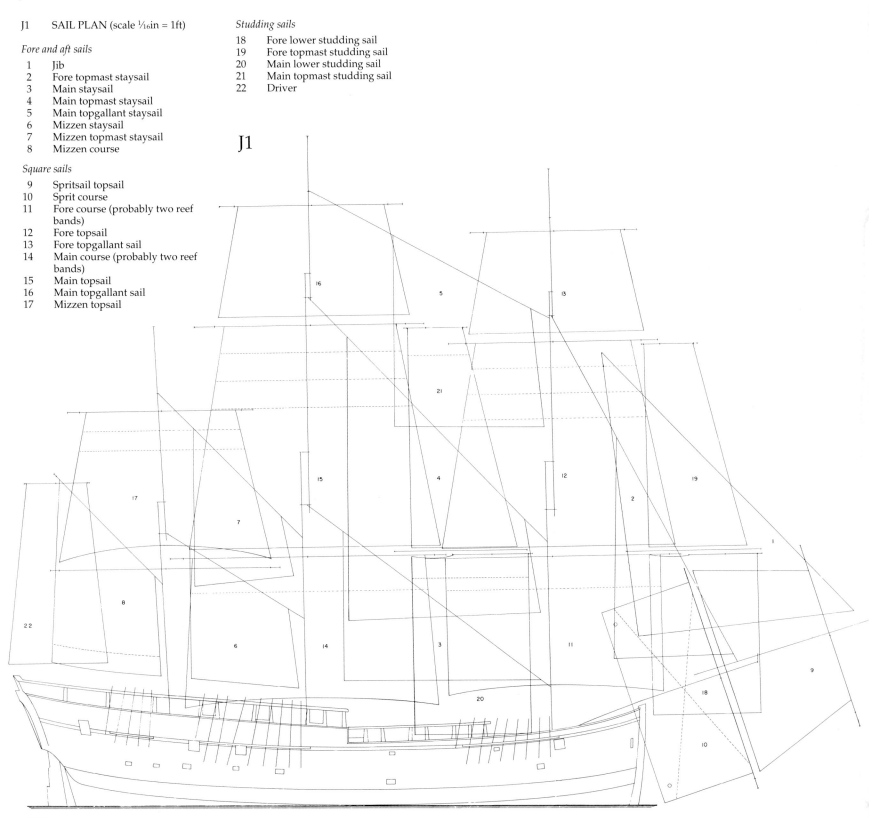

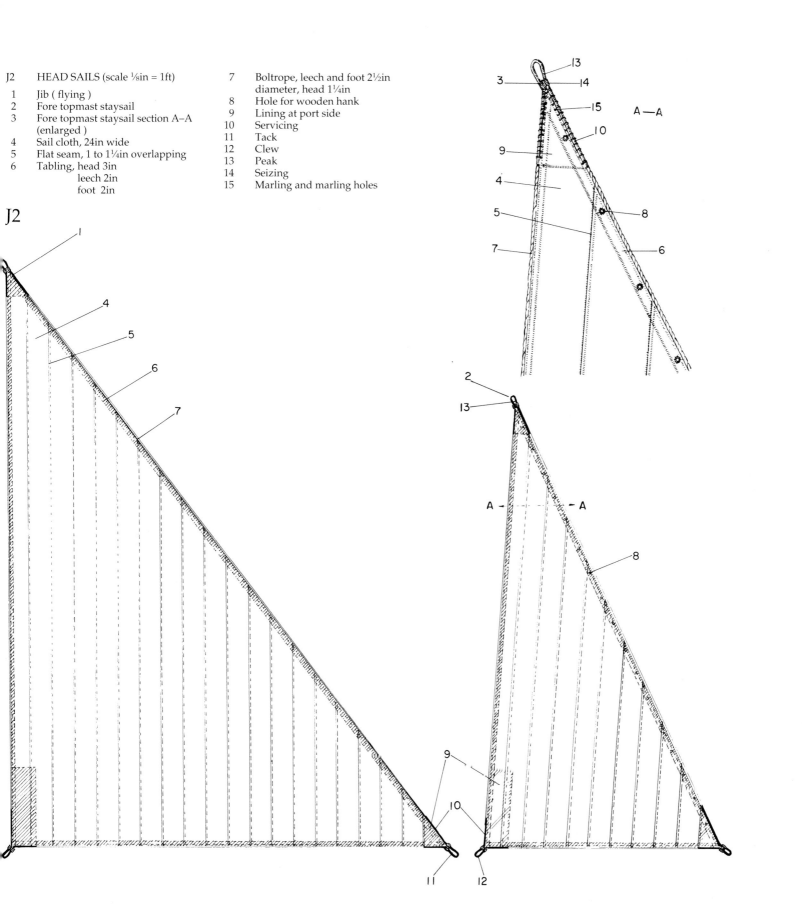

J2 HEAD SAILS (scale ⅛in = 1ft)

1 Jib (flying)
2 Fore topmast staysail
3 Fore topmast staysail section A–A
 (enlarged)
4 Sail cloth, 24in wide
5 Flat seam, 1 to 1¼in overlapping
6 Tabling, head 3in
 leech 2in
 foot 2in

7 Boltrope, leech and foot 2½in
 diameter, head 1¼in
8 Hole for wooden hank
9 Lining at port side
10 Servicing
11 Tack
12 Clew
13 Peak
14 Seizing
15 Marling and marling holes

J2

A — A

J Sails

J3/1 *Mainmast staysails*

1 Main staysail
2 Main topmast staysail
3 Main topgallant staysail
4 Peak
5 Nock earing
6 Tack
7 Clew
8 Aft leech
9 Head or stay
10 Mast leech or bunt
11 Foot
12 Lead thimble (sewn to leech rope)
13 Wooden hank
14 Stay running wooden hanks (sewn to head tabling)

J3/1

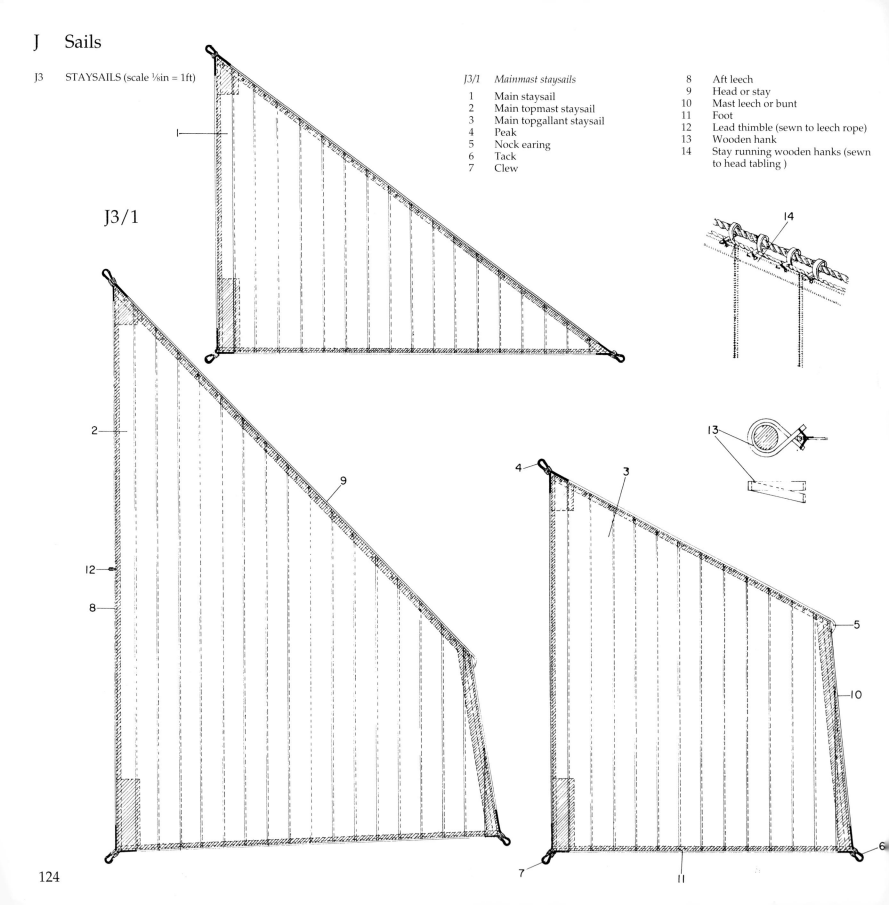

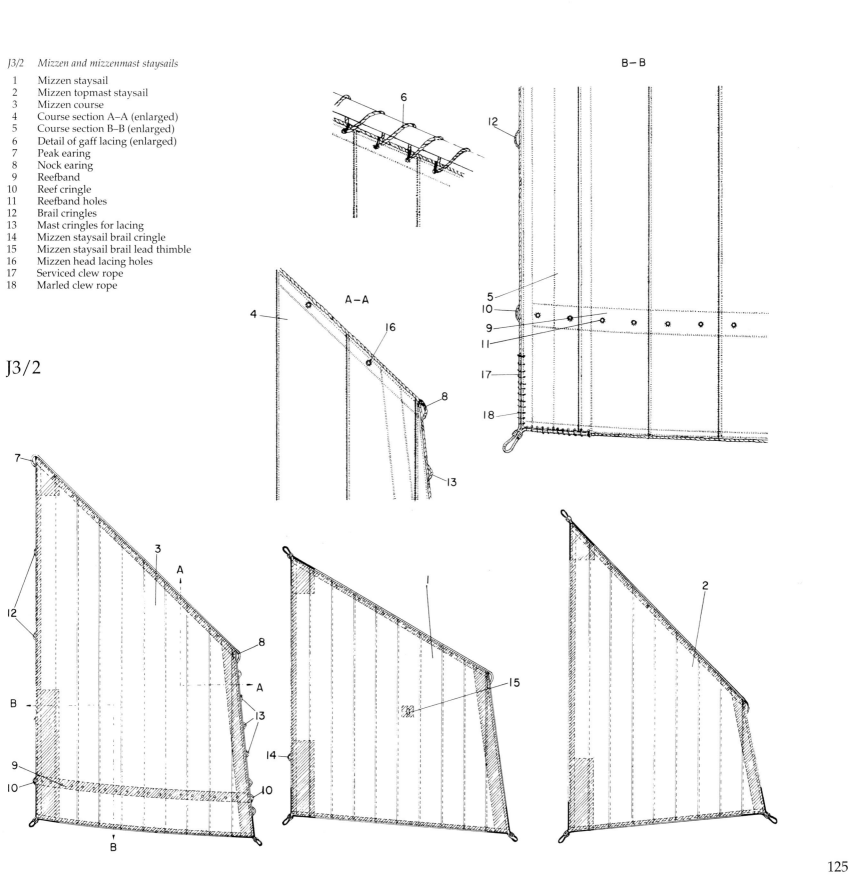

J3/2   *Mizzen and mizzenmast staysails*

1   Mizzen staysail
2   Mizzen topmast staysail
3   Mizzen course
4   Course section A–A (enlarged)
5   Course section B–B (enlarged)
6   Detail of gaff lacing (enlarged)
7   Peak earing
8   Nock earing
9   Reefband
10   Reef cringle
11   Reefband holes
12   Brail cringles
13   Mast cringles for lacing
14   Mizzen staysail brail cringle
15   Mizzen staysail brail lead thimble
16   Mizzen head lacing holes
17   Serviced clew rope
18   Marled clew rope

J3/2

B–B

A–A

J   Sails

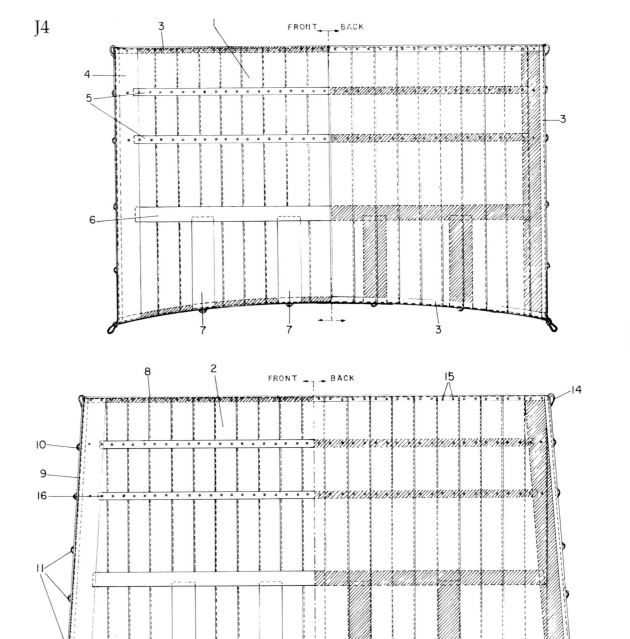

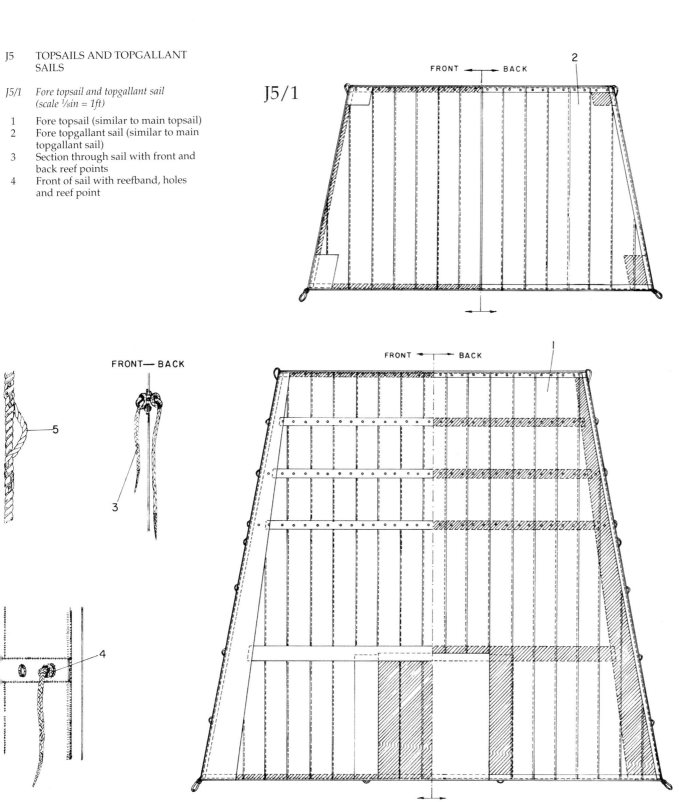

J5 TOPSAILS AND TOPGALLANT SAILS

J5/1 Fore topsail and topgallant sail (scale ⅛in = 1ft)

1 Fore topsail (similar to main topsail)
2 Fore topgallant sail (similar to main topgallant sail)
3 Section through sail with front and back reef points
4 Front of sail with reefband, holes and reef point

J5/1

FRONT — BACK

J   Sails

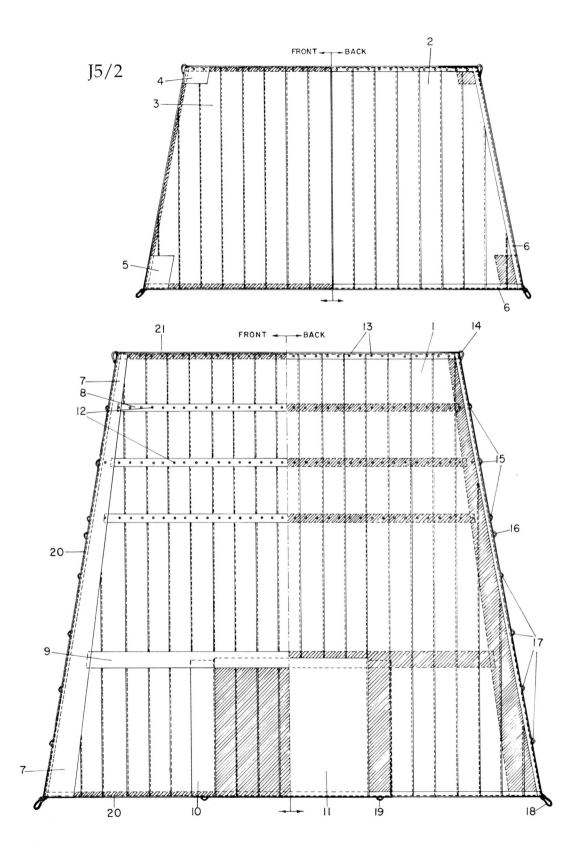

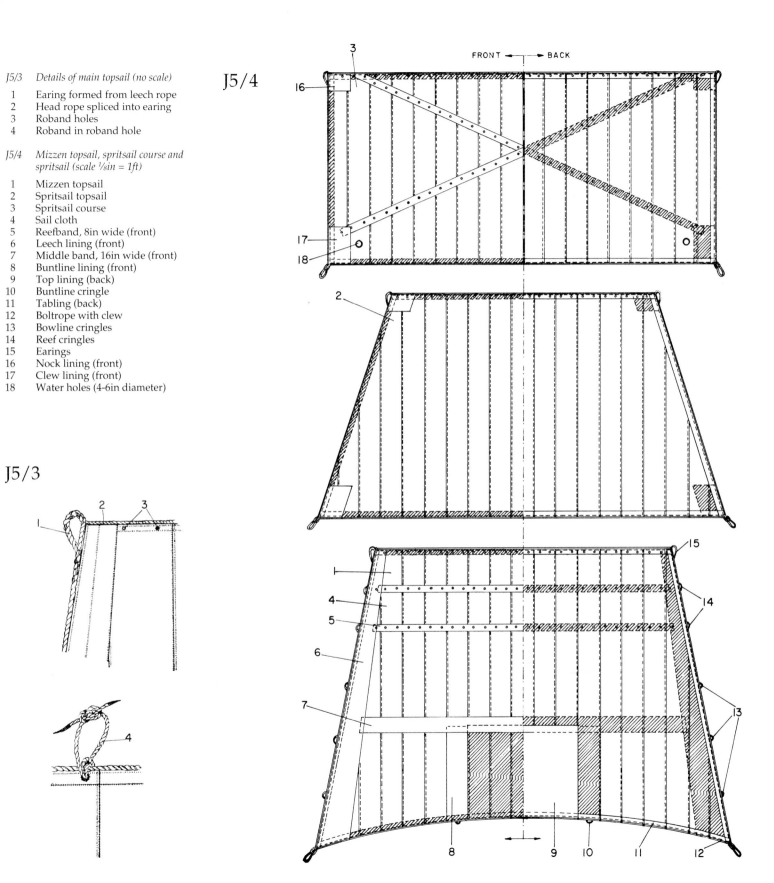

J5/3 Details of main topsail (no scale)

1 Earing formed from leech rope
2 Head rope spliced into earing
3 Roband holes
4 Roband in roband hole

J5/4 Mizzen topsail, spritsail course and spritsail (scale ⅛in = 1ft)

1 Mizzen topsail
2 Spritsail topsail
3 Spritsail course
4 Sail cloth
5 Reefband, 8in wide (front)
6 Leech lining (front)
7 Middle band, 16in wide (front)
8 Buntline lining (front)
9 Top lining (back)
10 Buntline cringle
11 Tabling (back)
12 Boltrope with clew
13 Bowline cringles
14 Reef cringles
15 Earings
16 Nock lining (front)
17 Clew lining (front)
18 Water holes (4-6in diameter)

J5/4

J5/3

J Sails

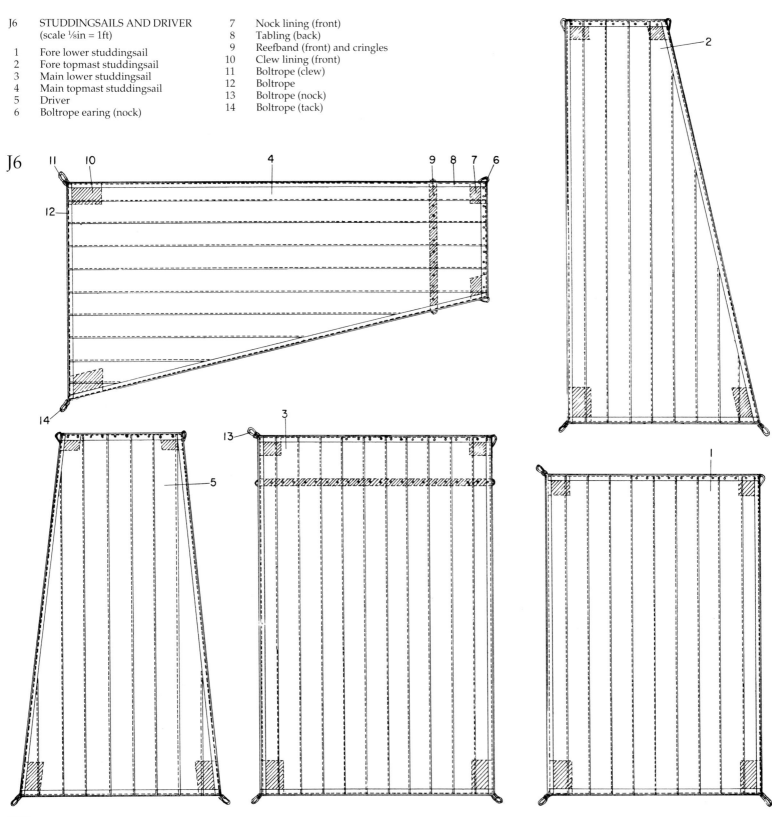

K Ship's boats

K1 LONGBOAT

K1/1 Carvel-built longboat (scale ³/₁₆in = 1ft)

1 After body lines, stern with built-in davit roll
2 Fore body lines with port side cable cleat (starboard side see 19)
3 Rudder and tiller
4 Sternpost
5 Transom knee
6 Sternson
7 Stern-sheets bench
8 Footwaling
9 Keelson
10 Gunwale
11 Mainmast step
12 Mainmast bracket and clamp
13 Thwart knee
14 Windlass
15 Tholes
16 Spaced footwaling
17 Loose thwart
18 Futtock
19 Bowsprit collar
20 Wales
21 Stem
22 Keel
23 Foremast bracket and clamp
24 Fixed thwart with knee
25 Apron
26 Halfbreadth lines

K1/2 Longboat with 2-masted sliding gunter rig (scale ⅛in = 1ft)

1 Sliding gunter sail
2 Blockmast
3 Sliding topmast
4 Double hoop for sliding topmast heel
5 Mast hoops
6 Topmast halyard
7 Sheet
8 Backstay
9 Lacing
10 Jib halyard
11 Flying jib
12 Jib sheets
13 Bowsprit
14 Jib tack

K1/3 Longboat with 2-masted spritsail rig (scale ⅛in = 1ft)

1 Sprit
2 Spritsail
3 Topping lift
4 Mast
5 Lacing
6 Spritsail halyard
7 Snotter
8 Vangs
9 Brails
10 Sheet
11 Backstay
12 Tack
13 Fore stay

K1/4 Longboat with 3-masted square/spritsail rig (scale ⅛in = 1ft)

1 Jiggermast
2 Mainmast
3 Foremast
4 Outrigger
5 Squaresail yard
6 Squaresail
7 Halyard
8 Sling parrel
9 Braces
10 Sheets

K1/1

K1/2

K1/3

K1/4

131

K Ship's boats

K2 PINNACE

K2/1 Carvel-built pinnace (scale ³⁄₁₆in = 1ft)

1   After body lines
2   Fore body lines
3   Rudder with an iron tiller
4   Cockpit
5   Stern-sheets bench
6   Footwaling
7   Tholes
8   Mainmast bracket and clamp
9   Spaced footwaling
10   Thwart
11   Futtock
12   Foremast bracket and clamp
13   Iron knee band
14   Halfbreadth lines

K2/2 Pinnace with 2-masted sliding gunter rig (scale ¹⁄₈in = 1ft)

K2/3 Pinnace with 2-masted settee rig (scale ¹⁄₈in = 1ft)

1   Settee yard
2   Settee sail
3   Peak halyard
4   Halyard
5   Tack
6   Reef point
7   Lacing
8   Bowline
9   Backstay
10   Vangs
11   Sheet

K2/4 Pinnace with single-masted spritsail rig (scale ¹⁄₈in = 1ft)

K2/1

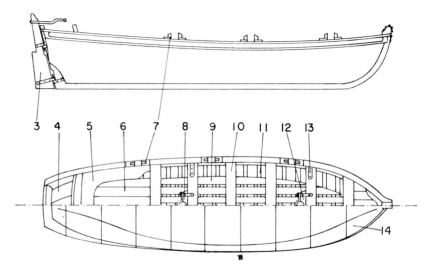

K2/2

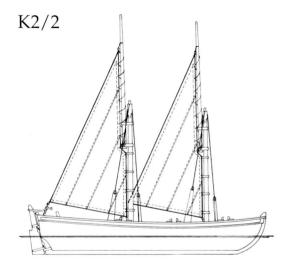

K2/3

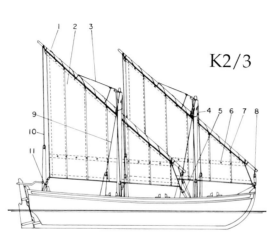

K2/4

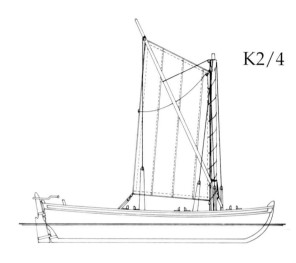

K3/1

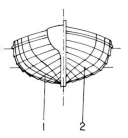

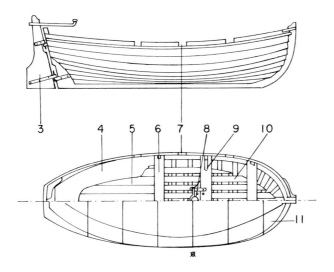

K3/2

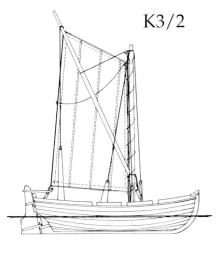

K3   YAWL

K3/1   Clinker-built yawl (scale ³/₁₆in = 1ft)

1   After body lines
2   Fore body lines
3   Rudder with tiller
4   Stern-sheets bench
5   Footwaling
6   Thwart
7   Row locks
8   Mast bracket and clamp
9   Thwart knee
10   Spaced footwaling
11   Halfbreadth lines

*K3/2   Yawl with single-masted spritsail rig
        (scale ¹/₈in = 1ft)*

K   Ship's boats

K4   SKIFF

K4/1   Clinker-built skiff (scale ³/₁₆in = 1ft)

1   After body lines
2   Fore body lines
3   Rudder with tiller yoke
4   Planked stern
5   Stern-sheets bench
6   Footwaling
7   Mast bracket and clamp
8   Spaced footwaling
9   Thwart
10   Planked bow
11   Halfbreadth lines

*K4/2   Skiff with single-masted squaresail rig
(scale ⅛in = 1ft)*

K5   BOAT EQUIPMENT (no scale)

1   Fender
2   Boat's oar
3   Skiff's oar or scull
4   Boat's hook
5   Bailer
6   Grapnel

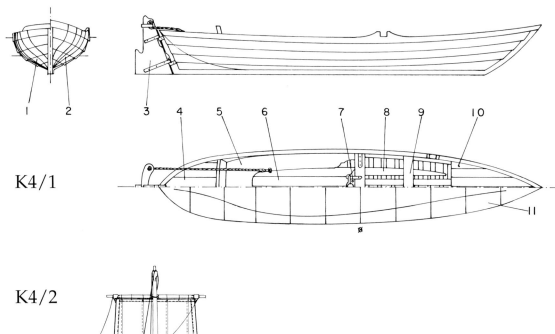

K4/1

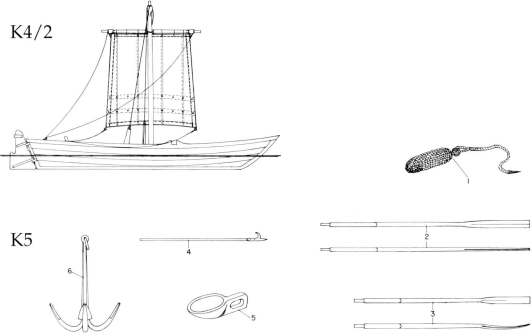

K4/2

K5

K6   BOAT STOWAGE ON DECK
(scale ³⁄₁₆in = 1ft)

K6/1   Top = port, bottom = starboard

1   Reserve spar
2   Quarterdeck spar gallows
3   Yawl
4   Fore hatch spar gallows
5   Quarterdeck
6   Upper deck
7   Main hatchway coaming
8   Middle chock
9   Longboat
10   Gripe
11   Fore hatchway coaming
12   Hood
13   Boat lashed to the reserve spars
14   Mr Banks' skiff
15   Pinnace
16   Two gripes lashed in the centre
17   Gripe with one-sided lashing

K6/1

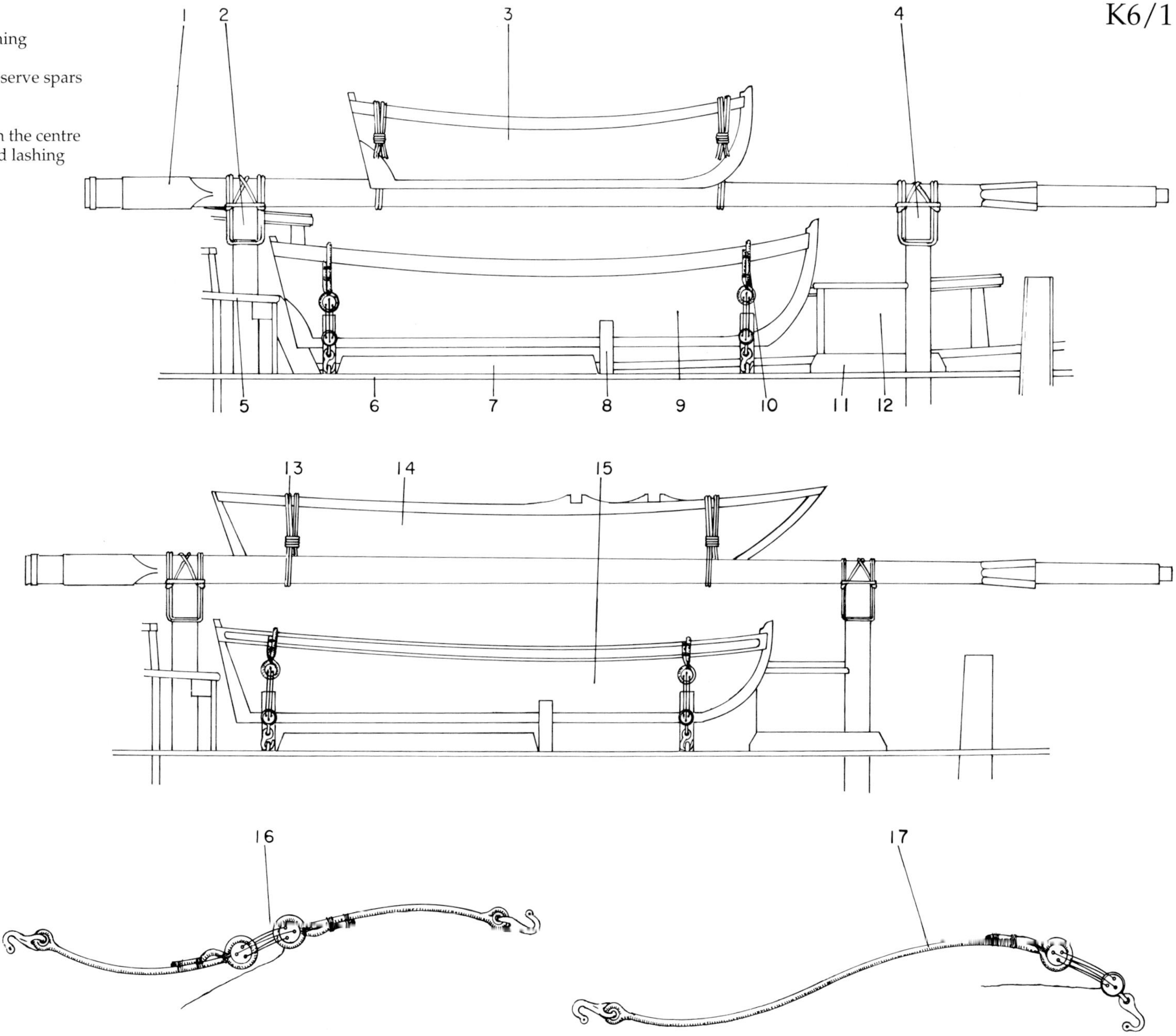

K Ship's boats

K6/2

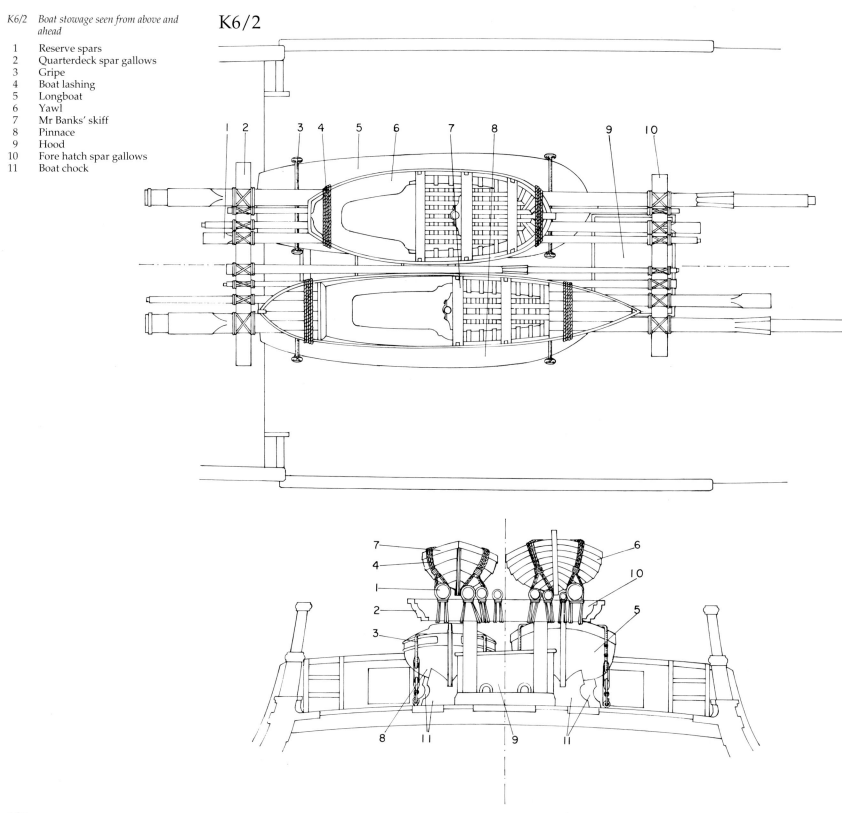